Studying Abroad

Studying Abroad

This book is part of the Peter Lang Education list.
Every volume is peer reviewed and meets
the highest quality standards for content and production.

PETER LANG
New York • Bern • Berlin
Brussels • Vienna • Oxford • Warsaw

Studying Abroad

What We Didn't See Coming

Beth D. Tolley, Editor

PETER LANG

New York • Bern • Berlin
Brussels • Vienna • Oxford • Warsaw

Library of Congress Cataloging-in-Publication Data

Names: Tolley, Beth D., editor.
Title: Studying abroad: what we didn't see coming / edited by Beth D. Tolley.
Description: New York: Peter Lang, 2018.
Includes bibliographical references and index.
Identifiers: LCCN 2018013306 | ISBN 978-1-4331-5096-8 (hardback: alk. paper)
ISBN 978-1-4331-5097-5 (paperback: alk. paper)
ISBN 978-1-4331-5691-5 (ebook pdf)
ISBN 978-1-4331-5692-2 (epub) | ISBN 978-1-4331-5693-9 (mobi)
Subjects: LCSH: Foreign study—Anecdotes.
Classification: LCC LB2375.S79 | DDC 370.116/2—dc23
LC record available at https://lccn.loc.gov/2018013306
DOI 10.3726/b13837

Bibliographic information published by **Die Deutsche Nationalbibliothek**.
Die Deutsche Nationalbibliothek lists this publication in the "Deutsche
Nationalbibliografie"; detailed bibliographic data are available
on the Internet at http://dnb.d-nb.de/.

The paper in this book meets the guidelines for permanence and durability
of the Committee on Production Guidelines for Book Longevity
of the Council of Library Resources.

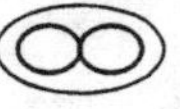

© 2018 Peter Lang Publishing, Inc., New York
29 Broadway, 18th floor, New York, NY 10006
www.peterlang.com

This book is dedicated to the city of Modena, Italy. Nestled in Italy's Po Valley, it is a vibrant city known for its culture, enogastronomy, world-class automobiles and a variety of industries. Modena is home to Bel Canto, and Pavarotti. It is the land of tortellini, balsamic vinegar, lambrusco, Ferrari, Maserati, and Lamborghini. For one month each year it is home for University of Georgia study abroad students who venture there to discover new families, new friends, new experiences, and new perspectives of a much larger world. The Modenese unselfishly open their city, their homes, their schools, and their hearts and embrace these American strangers who have set off on adventures of a lifetime. For all that Modena has given my students and me, it is only fitting that this book be dedicated to this enchanting city.

Contents

Foreword

For many years college faculty and administrators have known and promoted the many benefits of study-abroad programs. Whether extending a few weeks, a quarter, a semester, or even a full year, such programs often serve as students' first international experiences. When designed well, they broaden horizons, awaken cultural understanding, and add profoundly to the intended curriculum.

When my colleague, Dr. Beth Tolley, resurrected a study abroad program at the University of Georgia a decade ago, she expected much the same outcomes as those touted in other programs. *Studying Abroad: What We Didn't See Coming* describes that program, but reports more importantly on unexpected outcomes. The UGA/Modena Schools Study Abroad Program differed in some important ways from many other programs, and it was those differences that contributed the most to create those things we didn't see coming.

The standard study-abroad program takes a college course, or usually a set of college courses, the students who would take those courses, and one or more of the faculty who ordinarily teach those courses, and transplants them temporarily on a campus or a center in another country. For example, a French language department might offer the opportunity for advanced language students to take two or three of their French courses in a French-speaking country. They would thereby have more opportunities to practice the language in authentic settings and simultaneously experience more profoundly the cultural setting of the language and literature. In some programs, students may also take one or more courses at the host institution and transfer the credits to their own program.

The program created by Dr. Tolley and colleagues in Modena, Italy, was designed specifically for University of Georgia students who intended to become teachers, and particularly, but not exclusively, teachers in Early Childhood Education settings. Modena—readers will recognize Modena as the home of balsamic vinegar—was chosen to host the program not for its cuisine, though that is outstanding, but because Modena is located in Emilia Romagna, the Italian region famous internationally for its path-breaking approaches to early childhood education. The central goal, then, was to introduce to early childhood education students, in the most authentic way possible, the best thinking and practices in their chosen profession.

What makes the program unique; however, is that the students do not go to study Reggio ideas of practices academically. On the contrary, they go to live Reggio. With the close cooperation and collaboration with education professionals in Modena, known as Victoria Language and Culture, the students are placed in classrooms throughout Modena. To the extent possible, they are placed at levels that correspond to their interests, so that those teacher education students who are not specifically interested in early childhood education may be placed in, say, a middle-school setting instead. No matter what level, however, they will all experience the Reggio approach to education, either directly or, at higher grades, more indirectly.

The university students are not placed in the schools to be observers, to sit in the back of the classroom watching the teachers and students. Rather, they are expected, even directed, to be participants, co-teachers with the classroom teachers, even though, importantly, almost none of the scores of students who have participated in the program have any Italian language experience; most have little foreign language experience. They had to learn to communicate and participate in ways not dissimilar to what many children in American schools experience – the discomfort of being the outsider, the language learner, the one not in the know.

At the same time, the program placed students, individually, with Italian families. Placing them individually was an important part of the process: we (for I had the great privilege of being selected to serve as co-director with Dr. Tolley until my retirement) knew that if students were placed in pairs or groups, they would be disinclined to enter fully into the cultural life of the families, preferring to spend time in the refuge of themselves. Our only concession was to select only families who had at least one member who spoke English. Thus between the classroom placements and the family placements, the students experienced a full baptism in learning to learn anew.

During the semester immediately preceding the study-abroad experience, the participants, Dr. Tolley, and I met four or five times for a few hours to talk about logistics and expectations but especially about what they might plan to teach, given the considerable constrains of the language barrier. By the second or third meeting, they each knew the level they were assigned to and most had seen pictures of their classroom and had exchanged rudimentary greetings with the children with whom they would be working. From that, and their academic study of education, they imagined a curriculum they could deliver—American foods, family life in Italy and the US, and so on. During our time in Modena, we held weekly seminars after school, spending part of the time debriefing but insisting on spending a good deal of time in focused, academic inquiry into the dramatic differences in childhood between two cultures, or the contrasts between Reggio schools and the schools they had experienced in the US, or the historical determinants of diverging social and political structures.

Teacher education programs are typically time-intensive, making it difficult to carve out a full semester for a study-abroad program. At the University of Georgia, for example, students spend their first two years completing most of their university general education requirements. Each of the following four semesters includes mandatory practicum experiences in local classrooms, starting with guided observations and culminating in an entire semester-long internship as a student teacher. There simply is no space for a full semester abroad. As a result, our study-abroad program was four weeks long, scheduled at the very end of each spring semester, when Italian public schools were still in session. Consequently, participants experienced classrooms whose rituals and routines were well established, at a point in their own studies when there were no pressures from exams and assignments for other courses. They could focus entirely on what they were experiencing of childhood in an unfamiliar culture, of teaching in unfamiliar classrooms, and of their own learning in unfamiliar surroundings.

What follows, then, is a set of observations from a range of participants in the UGA/Modena Schools Study Abroad Program, all reflecting on what we didn't see coming when we signed on to this adventure. The participants represented here are not just the students, though their voices are central. The participants include as well the amazing Italian families who opened their doors (and, as it turned out, their hearts) to American university students. They include also the courageous Italian teachers who risked their precious instructional time (not to mention their precious students) to strangers from the US. And, of course, they include the women of Victoria Language and Culture, without whom, quite literally, this amazing study-abroad program could never have existed.

Every year that I had the privilege of working with UGA students in this study-abroad program, I saw the same thing happen to a score of bright, thoughtful, often frightened young university students, yet somehow I saw it anew, never seeing it coming until it happened. At our first few meetings, the students were excited, a bit nervous, full of the obvious questions – what if my hosts don't like me? How will we find our way around an Italian city? How can I teach children who do not understand me? As the weeks passed, the nervousness grew, the uncertainty mounted. At the Atlanta airport on departure day, there were tears in the eyes of the students and their families who had gathered to see them off, but mostly brave faces. But hours later, as the bus took us from Milano to Modena, anxiety became palpable. Dr. Tolley and I always leapt off the bus, eager to embrace old friends, but every year the students hung back, slow to step out and meet the strangers awaiting them, even though they had exchanged emails and photographs. But what I never saw coming, every year, was the amazing transformation in four weeks. As we gathered to take the bus back to Milano, a score of young university students wept to part from their new families, who wept with equal sadness. The score of students who boarded the bus were not the same people as those who descended from it four weeks before. They were wiser, deeper, and more mature, with greater understanding of life and learning. I suspect, as well, that they were prepared to be far better teachers, though I think I *did* see that coming.

Ron Butchart
Distinguished Research Professor, Emeritus
Former Head, Department of Educational Theory and Practice
University of Georgia

Preface

This book is composed of reflective writings from America students, Italian host families, and Italian teachers and administrators who comprise the core of the UGA/Modena Schools Study Abroad Program sponsored by the Department of Educational Theory and Practice at the University of Georgia. Offered predominantly to those seeking degrees in early childhood or middle grades education, the program has surpassed all initial beliefs of its impact, importance, and dynamics. It was organized for the purpose of exposing and educating pre-service teachers to the Reggio Emilia approach to early learning. This approach, originating after WWII in the province of Reggio Emilia, Italy, focuses on preschool and primary education. Fundamental to the approach is the belief that children form their own identities and personalities at an early age and learn through experiences in which relationships are fundamental. It is an innovative and inspiring approach that values the child as strong, capable and resilient. It stresses the belief that each child has potential and possesses a deep innate curiosity that drives his interest to understand his world and his place within it. It is from this perspective that my students observe, absorb and envision how such procedures and methods can be put into practice in their Common Core curriculum-driven American classrooms.

The program also offers the opportunity for American students to walk in the shoes of non-native speakers and develop empathy for the non-English speaking children they currently work with in their teacher preparation field experiences and for those who will enter their future classrooms. Houser (2008) describes developing empathy as one of the values of a "cultural plunge" for pre-service teachers. My students emerge from the program with a deeper understanding and first-hand knowledge of second language acquisition and the anxieties that arise when they find themselves often for the first time in the minority with very limited or no understanding of the dominant language. Such experiences help pre-service teachers "make connections between their own experiences and those of their future students" (Palmer & Menard-Warwick, 2012, p. 25). They are not unlike the student in a study by Palmer and Menard-Warwick (2012) who claimed that others in her teacher preparation program had done presentations or written reflections about second language acquisition, but she had lived it. Her reflections affirm that there's nothing like being there to make the learning authentic and meaningful. The opportunities for interactions among families and teachers "forces teacher candidates to experience cultural, pedagogical, and ideological dissonance, a sensation that promotes increased ideological awareness and clarity (Alfaro & Quezada, 2010, p. 50).

For four weeks American students live with Italian host families and work twenty hours a week in either an Italian pre-school, elementary, or middle school. They are immersed in the culture of Italy and become a member of their selected host family. Their daily activities revolve around their work in the schools and the routines and rituals of their families. They attend soccer games, communions, class parties, and family outings. They find ways to teach Basic English vocabulary, plan activities based on the class theme of the year, teach English songs and rhymes, and are rewarded with gleeful hugs and adoration. Host siblings are proud to brag about their "American sister" who teaches across the hall. My students become contributing members of their families and classrooms, and the experiences enable and encourage them to absorb and blend in with the culture. A case study by Garmon (2004) incorporating the reflections of a teacher candidate and mirroring the elements of the UGA/Modena program highlights "it was her intercultural experiences that actually stimulated her multicultural growth by pushing her out of her comfort zone" (p. 212). All of my students will attest to the hesitancy and then resultant impact of stepping outside their comfort zones only to realize that the terrain was not as frightening as they had perceived. Once the "coming out" is accomplished they are thrilled and measure their success of fleeing their comfort zones and the resulting discovery of the ability to blend in, by the number of times someone asks them for directions, by the gradual realization that they can easily navigate the cities, and by the sudden awareness that the sensations in the pits of their stomachs have disappeared.

I, too, experienced these ah-ha moments and relate completely to their feelings of accomplishment and self-efficacy. That day during the first year of the program when I found myself on the wrong bus, miles from my destination, shopping bags in each hand and patiently but exasperatingly attempting to explain to the bus driver who understood not one word of English that I needed to get home to Cognento, was a turning point. Navigating a city bus system would be a difficult endeavor for me even in Athens, GA. Adding the complexities of being totally lost with no language to communicate where I needed to be, with no iPhone with contacts and a GPS, and a frustrated bus driver who more than likely would have preferred to just leave me standing on the side of the road, made it, at the time, seem an insurmountable task. I still laugh about that adventure ... the most sensible reaction to unexpected predicaments that I didn't see coming. That experience has enabled me to understand completely the dilemmas that my students often find themselves in and makes my advice and empathy authentic, purposeful, and believable.

The home placements are the component that adds the most richness to the UGA/Modena Schools study abroad program. They enable students to become one with the culture and experience it first-hand rather than as a tourist. Study abroad programs that house students in dorms or group housing of some sort deprive them of many meaningful and rich experiences. There is something impactful about having a host brother joyfully give up his room for a month, about learning to prepare authentic Italian dishes with guidance from a host mother, about riding bikes to school with a host sister, and about realizing that the laundry hanging on the line includes some personal items that are your own. Families offer one of the first realizations of Italian culture when students find themselves surrounded by the constant chatter.

> Too much, some might say. OK, but at least they talk. In the English-speaking world, many families communicate via adhesive notes on the refrigerator. Everyone has his or her own separate life, and grabs something to eat in between attending courses and meetings at school. Not in Italy. Around Italian tables, people reason, argue, and learn to defend (or change) their points of view. (Severgnini, 2006, p.52)

And a number one rule of every Italian family is that everyone sits down at the table together.

These life-changing home placements are diligently thought out and determined by the very capable staff of Victoria Language and Culture, directed by Roberta Rinaldi and Anna Giovannini. Information gathered from students and potential host families is thoroughly reviewed and compared in order to determine the best possible matches. Families are carefully screened and interviewed to ascertain those best suited for each individual participant. Some families request to host each year, some vary their participation from year to year, and others are first time hosts. Regardless, each year of the program the students overwhelmingly rate the host families as the most influential and valuable aspect of the program.

And each year, unfortunately, there are many more willing host families than there are American student participants.

For most the relationship that begins the day they step off the chartered bus in Modena to greet a family they have only met through emails and Skype visits who is waving American flags and welcome signs, grows exponentially over the four-week period, and they find themselves anticipating and planning for trips and reunions to follow. Some included stories in the book recall and describe those reunions. They consider their host families new family and ones they will remember and stay in touch with long after their return to the U.S.

Similar thought and consideration is given to securing school placements. Teachers are recruited and informed of the expectations and responsibilities. Students offer grade preferences and are matched with teachers in this way. Attention is also given to place students in schools attended by host siblings in order to create a more realistic daily routine for host families and more authentic routine for the American students. Pre-departure sessions on campus focus on classroom information sent by their assigned host teachers, and work begins prior to departure on the activities and resources to implement and use in the Italian classrooms. Students prepare an "all about me" video to share with their Italian classes, and the final hook is the emailed letters and photographs they receive from the children in their host classrooms. I was amused by one letter from a group of 5-year-olds who reported that "they were 13 boys and 12 girls" who liked to sing and draw and dance. They assured their American student that they did not expect any gifts from her … "they would love her just the same." However, if she decided she wanted to bring something to them "they liked crayons and bubbles." I continue to be mesmerized by the honesty and spontaneity of the Italian children. Their confidence assures me that they will go far in life.

Classroom experiences are enhanced by excursions to various educational centers that further emphasize the Italian attention to children and families. The Italian culture truly embraces the idea "it takes a village" and provides support for children and families in a variety of ways. A special excursion is the tour of Reggio Children, a center in the town of Reggio Emilia that highlights the beginnings of the Reggio method and its essential elements. In keeping with the idea of reciprocity of learning, I frequently meet with Italian teachers interested in learning and understanding more about the American education system and hearing about a typical day in an American school.

Also included in the program are numerous visits of cultural and historical interest. The masterpieces in the Uffici, the majesty of the David, the charisma of the Venetian gondoliers, the ancient churches in every town and village and the buzz surrounding their piazzas add to the cultural understanding of the country and enhance insight into the dynamics of the Italian families and their priorities.

My students find themselves in awe of the magnificence of the architecture of the cathedrals, piazzas, homes, and government buildings. The first views of the Grande Canal in Venice and the Tuscan hillsides leave them all speechless.

As pre-service teachers my students soon realize that these important aspects of Italian life and culture are imbedded in the curriculum of the schools and often drive the curriculum. The national pride is ever present in day-to-day life and in the schools as information is explored and experienced through what the Reggio approach asserts are the "one hundred languages" of children. An understanding and an appreciation for the architecture, history, and the elements of everyday life that are fundamental in an Italian education range from the broader knowledge of simply recognizing the Roman Coliseum to the most minute hands-on-lesson of mixing just the right paint colors to capture the ripeness of the tomatoes in the school garden.

This academic program for soon-to-be teachers learning and exploring a different approach to early learning and teaching transforms into an opportunity for learning and growth in unexpected ways and alters all who choose to participate. It ignites in all the significance of travel. Each year some remain in Europe and travel with family and friends. Others plan return trips to further their travels, reunite with the host families, work as au pairs, or work as counselors in the summer camp sponsored by Victoria Language.

This edited collection of essays that started out as a guide for cultural study and exploration abroad has emerged as tales of personal discovery, maturation, wonder, and the impact of relationships. The first person accounts of fears, thrills, and ah-ha moments grab the reader, pull him into the experiences and appeal to his range of emotions. "For it is the students themselves who are the most articulate sources of information about the value of study abroad …" (Hopkins, 1999, p. 3). The book highlights the bonds of unexpected friendships, illustrates the effects of human kindness, offers testimonials to the flexibility of the human spirit, and illuminates the fact that we live in a world without borders. It is an effort to document what we didn't see coming.

References

Alfaro, C., & Quezada, R. L. (2010). International teacher professional development: Teacher reflections of authentic teaching and learning experience. *Teaching Education, 21*(1), 47–59.

Garmon, M. A. (2004). Changing preservice teachers' attitudes/beliefs about diversity. *Journal of Teacher Education, 55*(3), 201–213.

Hopkins (1999). Studying abroad as a form of experiential education. *Liberal education, (85)*3, 36–45.

Houser (2008). Cultural plunge: A critical approach for multicultural development in teacher education. *Race, Ethnicity and Education, 11*(4), 465–482.

Palmer, D., & Menard-Warwick, J. (2012). Short-term study abroad for Texas preservice teachers: On the road from empathy to critical awareness. *Multicultural Education, 19*(3), 17–26.

Severgnini, B. (2006). *La bella figura: A field guide to the Italian mind*. New York: Broadway Books.

Acknowledgments

I must first acknowledge and offer my heart-felt thanks to those who have contributed their touching stories of reflection for this book. Without them there would be no manuscript. I am grateful that they chose to be a part of the study abroad program and have thoughtfully shared their memories and experiences with me. I am indebted, as well, to the 156 other students who have participated in the program over the nine years of its existence. Although they did not formally offer stories for the book, I hold special memories of times spent with them in Italy and have many undocumented stories in my mind of those things that they didn't see coming. To Roberta Rinaldi, Anna Giovannini and the amazing associates of Victoria Language and Culture I owe so very much. Their efforts make the entire UGA/Modena Schools Study Abroad Program possible. They are much more than colleagues. They are dear friends.

I am indebted to my "salon sisters" Dr. Cynthia Dillard, Dr. Morgan Faison, Dr. Jennifer Hauver, and Dr. Sonya Janis who were the first to listen to my idea for this book and encouraged me every step of way. I appreciate the monthly lunch conversations with Dr. Betty Knighton during which she shared her expertise on all things publishing and pointed me in all of the right directions. I am grateful to Dr. Ron Butchart for his years of dedication to the program as co-director and for his guidance as I began this venture of capturing the stories. To my best friend, Mickey Dillard Cain, I express gratitude for venturing with me on my maiden voyage to Italy. I hope she can return with me one day now that my international skills are a bit more refined and my mastering of the Italian language goes beyond the translation of "si."

I would be remiss without mentioning the support of Stephanie Bales. I can list few of my professional accomplishments in which she did not in some way play a critical part. Her knowledge of the original program that existed before my tenure at UGA was paramount in getting the UGA/Modena Schools program up and going. Crucial to my efforts, as well, was her brilliance for organizing and formatting the manuscript and understanding the "big picture" of all that was required.

Last but not least I must acknowledge my family … Edward and Spencer. They have graciously allowed me to physically leave their lives for one month each year and pursue adventures in Italy with my students and Italian friends. Their unselfish support and understanding were things I didn't see coming, and have enhanced the rewards of my endeavors.

Introduction

When the task of resurrecting and restoring my university department's defunct Italy study abroad program fell to me through the process of elimination, I underestimated the mission. I grossly underestimated the amount of time and effort involved in reestablishing and reinstating a study abroad program in a country I had never visited. Add to this the fact that I held a temporary lecturer position within my university department with no guarantee that I would even be employed when the program was ready to launch. Without the enthusiastic cooperation and pledge to serve as director-of-record from my friend and colleague, Dr. Ron Butchart, my efforts could have proved completely futile. Ron and his supportive wife, Amy, were instrumental in helping me stay focused on the task and establishing the rigor and reputation of the program in its early years.

Most contacts from the defunct program were outdated and the few viable contacts were uncooperative. Institutional requirements called for a totally revamped program proposal with multiple components all accompanied with sound rationales and country-specific information. Institutional officials never discouraged my efforts. They fully understood the institutional benefits of overseas educational experiences, among them improved academic performance among participants (Ingraham & Peterson, 2004; Malmgran & Galvin, 2008; Sutton & Rubin, 2004) and an attractive marketing tool (Dwyer & Peters, 2004). "At the university level it [studying abroad] has transcended its history as a grand tour for the leisure class and the more plebian junior year abroad (Bennett, 2009). Today's world requires that universities "influence students to become more socially responsible global citizens" (Caulfield & Woods, 2013, p. 31), and study abroad programs offer opportunities for such influence. Bennett (2009) claims that "exposure to cultural differences is broadening, and therefore a legitimate aspect of education in the modern world" (p. 1). Many U.S. colleges and university administrators consider study abroad programs "high-impact educational practice" (Kuh & Schneider, 2008). The dean of the College of Education at the time offered unwavering support for the program's renewal. As one of the largest colleges on the UGA campus and with the college's early childhood program being a high-demand major, he was concerned by the fact that the college had lost one of its few study abroad programs. Being able to offer more study abroad opportunities to students, and particularly to education majors, was a priority for him. He shared the belief that "… the institutional investment in study abroad programs can be more readily justified not only in terms of the benefits to participants, but also in terms of how study abroad relates to the greater common good" (Murphy, Sahakyan, Yong-Yi, & Magnan, 2014, p. 2).

At times overwhelmed by the list of requirements, I was nevertheless determined to honor my commitment and continued gathering bits and pieces of the old program and incorporating them with the new. Eighteen months into the process, the newly established program had institutional approval. Scheduled to begin in May 2009, the UGA/Modena Schools Study Abroad Program had its first sixteen University of Georgia student participants in place. Proud of my accomplishment and my tenacity in tackling this task, I was yet to realize the other aspects of my underestimations … other things I didn't see coming. Those things described by Gemignani (2009) as "happenstance events" (p. 162).

When I voluntarily agreed to bring back the program, I had given no thought to the impact that this international experience would have on me. My views of the world, its people, and cultures have broadened dramatically. I have been forced out of my comfort zone on multiple occasions and in so doing have learned a great deal about my abilities, my determination, natural survival skills, and the multiple facets of language. I have gained appreciation for my family who understand my commitment to this program even though it separates us for a month each year. I have formed international friendships that are stronger than many I have with childhood classmates. I have underestimated the significance of so many aspects of life and have taken stock of my priories. Each year upon my return to Italy I am reminded of many of those priorities and for that month begin to relax and become reenergized by the slower-paced Italian life style. My long-term memory holds the valuable lessons that I have learned from my Italian experiences over the years.

An equally significant underestimation of my endeavors was the impact of the UGA/Modena Schools Program on my students, the Italian families and the Italian teachers. It has taken eight years of reflection for me to fully see the power of this international experience and how lives are changed because of it. "[S]tudy abroad experiences can be significantly shaped by happenstance, and these accidental factors, especially when they contribute to the development of a connection with people, moved to the center of how students construct the meaning of their entire experience" (Gemignani, 2009, p. 162). My delayed realizations further the research of Paige, Fry, Stallman, Josic and Jon (2009) that highlights the long-term impact of cultural exchange experiences. While their data focuses on the long-term effects on student participants, it offers implications for the same long-term effects on program directors and other stakeholders. My life is certainly enriched because of all of the wonderful people—students, families, and teachers—who have been a part of it. There is great satisfaction in knowing that I have helped facilitate life-changing opportunities. "Intercultural learning can be both an immediate and long-term effect of exchange. In the short term, intercultural learning involves the acquisition of intercultural sensitivity and the ability to exercise intercultural competence in the exchange culture. A middle-term effect is the transfer of intercultural sensitivity and potential competence from the exchange culture to other cultural contexts. The longer-term effects involve the development of global citizenship and/or other manifestations of a permanently heightened awareness and appreciation of cultural difference" (Bennett, 2009, p. 4).

My underestimation of the far-reaching effects of the UGA/Modena Schools Study Abroad Program was the impetus that pushed me to gather reflective narratives into a book as a way to share personal accounts of growth, change, adventure, and learning. The stories support the survey results of the Institute for the International Education of Students confirming the idea that study abroad positively and indisputably influences the career path, world-view, and self-confidence of those who participate (Dwyer & Peters, 2004). The selected essays are representative of the 170 students, the 170 families, and the 539 teachers who have participated in the study abroad program over nine years. Their personal narratives speak to the impact of the experience on their lives—then and now. While each came away with unique memories, all share common lessons learned. It is important to note that only three of the essays were submitted by students who had participated in the program within the last two years. The others came from students more than two years removed from the experience. They offer evidence as to the long-term and lasting impact of study abroad on the enrichment of participants' lives.

Replicating the findings of Paige et al. (2009), Gemignani (2009), Hopkins (1999) McLeod, and Wainwright (2009), and Zhao, Meyers, and Meyers (2009), domains or themes emerged from the personal stories. In my initial planning for the book this was my anticipation and hope. Weeks into reading the narratives, the words began to speak of Hope, Discovery, Inspiration, Acceptance, Subtleties, and Collaboration. These themes became the major parts of the book with appropriate narratives offering testimonials to each theme. As in Gemignani's (2009) work "the themes are not present in all cases, and where they are evident they occur in varying degrees" (p. 166). They do, however, encompass the words and language of the contributors and are well grounded in what was actually described about their experiences.

It is important to make clear that a specific and content-anticipated prompt was not given to the contributors. They were simply asked to write a roughly 3000 word reflection of their study abroad experience and what it had meant to them. All essays were voluntarily submitted, and while ultimately positive in nature, are sprinkled with remembered moments of uneasiness, anxiety, and possible doom. One study highlights that as many as 84% of participants report of the positive impact of a study abroad experience even as many as 50 years later (Paige et al., 2009). Gemignani (2009), through case vignettes of study abroad experiences, notes that,

> students' stories are compelling. They present a window onto amazing experiences and onto the very personal ways that those experiences were understood. The case vignettes show that sometimes the study abroad experience can be more than another experience abroad. It can be profound. (pp. 162–163)

Murphy-Lejeune (2002) explains that the affective and cognitive disorientation that we label "culture shock" is in fact "the necessary lever which pries open individuals in their search for shared meaning" (p. 133).

Although all submitted essays ultimately portray rewarding experiences, I would be naïve to believe that this study abroad program over the years did not leave some participants disappointed and disillusioned. I must emphasize, however, that none of this nature or with this message were received, and invitations to be a part of this reflective book were distributed to every student who had participated over the eight years. This cannot be said about the Italian participants. Because of the large number of Italian parents, teachers and school administrators who have been a part of the program throughout its entirety, it was not possible or feasible to extend the invitation to reflect on the experience to all 570 Italian participants. The associates of Victoria Language and Culture extended the writing opportunity to a random group of parents, teachers, and administrators in hopes of assembling a representative group. The variety in their writings assures me that this was, indeed, accomplished.

It is only fitting that the bulk of my contributions to this book project were written while in Italy with group #9. The sea of tiled roofs, the church bell concertos, the view of the lush gardens of the Canalgrande Hotel from its sprawling terrace, the elderly couples strolling arm-in-arm with no apparent destination in mind, the haphazard driving techniques of Italian motorists, the 24/7 aroma of bolognese sauce simmering from random Italian kitchens, squealing Italian children who are seldom hushed, along with an abundance of other rich happenings and sensations helped me capture the essence of beautiful Italia and encouraged me to incorporate the richness of my surroundings into my words.

> Italy is a soft drug peddled in predictable packages, such as hills in the sunset, olive groves, lemon trees, white wine, and raven-haired girls … It's the kind of place that can have you fuming and then purring in the space of a hundred meters … Italy is the only workshop in the world that can turn out both Botticellis and Berlusconis. People who live in Italy say they want to get out, but those who do escape all want to come back. (Severgnini, 2006, pp. 2–3)

For all that Italy and its wonderful people have shared with my students and me, we hope our words do justice to their influence and impressions they have made on our lives. Qualitative studies endorse the richness and impact of study abroad programs in which the students feel they have established a strong connection to the people and places of their host culture (Bond, Koont, & Stephenson 2005; Gemignani 2009). Gemignani's (2009) findings explain these connections occur through the idea of "being there" which exemplifies the totality of the cultural immersion.

At the same time, my students and I draw great satisfaction from knowing that in some unexpected way we have changed the lives of the Italian families and teachers as evidenced by their written testimonials. Submitted in Italian, they have been carefully translated so as to maintain the essence of the language and sentence composition and to preserve the cultural nuances. Research explores the various aspects of American students studying abroad and its impact on their lives, but few studies focus on and highlight the impact made on the international hosts and stakeholders. Their contributions to the book offer a glimpse into this reciprocity and emphasize the realization that the experience is certainly one of a rich and complete two-way cultural exchange.

Walt Whitman (1885) wrote of the child who went forth one day, and everything he saw he became for that day or "for a part of the day, or for many years..." (p. 118). Each of us, regardless of nationality, who has participated in this cultural exchange program, is not unlike the child in Whitman's poem. We have gone forth and we have become so much of what we saw. We are changed—our lives rearranged, because for four short weeks we embraced a unique experience and united with strangers that we felt we had known for many years. All can attest to the fact that the length of time abroad was not as important as the actual experience. Even short-term programs promote intellectual, social and personal development (Chamberlain, 2009; Gonyea, 2008) and create opportunities for life-long learning and relationships. Gerald Fry asserts that "if it's done right, if it's done with intensity of learning, a short-term program can have impact" (Fischer, 2009). I join the league of study abroad directors who argue that such an experience is transformative.

However, one missing element for me over the years has been a way to adequately describe the power and the significant influence imbedded in and radiating from this study abroad opportunity. I can easily describe the work that will be done, the month-long itinerary, how families and schools are determined, the methodologies that will be observed in the classrooms, and the deliciousness of the Italian fare. But words to describe the gripping impact and the appropriate mindset have escaped me ... until now. These poignant tales of what no one saw coming will more than adequately prepare future participants—both American and Italian—for what lies ahead in the adventure. *Studying abroad: What we didn't see coming* will entertain and draw new participants and casual readers into the lives of thirty three unsuspecting adventurers and showcase the wonders that life offers when least expected.

References

Bennett, M. J. (2009). Defining, measuring, and facilitating intercultural learning: A conceptual introduction to the *Intercultural Education* double supplement. *Intercultural Education, 20*(1–2), 1–13.

Bond, L., Koont, S., & Stephenson, S. (2005). The power of being there: Study abroad in Cuba and promotion of a "culture of peace." *Frontiers: The interdisciplinary Journal of Study Abroad, 8,* 113–142.

Caulfield, J., & Woods, T. (2013). Experiential learning: Exploring its long-term impact on socially responsible behavior. *Journal of the Scholarship of Teaching and Learning, 13*(2), 31–48.

Chamberlain, T. (2009). *Using high impact practices to maximize student gains.* http://nsse.indiana.edu/webinars/TuesdaysWithNSSE/2009_06_23_High_Impact/High%20Impact%20Practices%202009-05-23_v2003.pdf

Dwyer, M., & Peters, C. (2004). The benefits of study abroad: Study confirms significant gains. *Transitions Abroad.* Retrieved from: http://www.transitionsabroad.com/publications/magazine/0403/benefits_study_abroad.shtml

Fischer, K. (2009). Short study-abroad trips can have lasting effect, research suggests. *The Chronicle of Higher Education.* Retrieved from: http://chronicle.com/daily/2009/02/12191n.htm

Gemignani, C. L. (2009). *Understanding the study abroad experience of university students.* (Graduate thesis dissertation, Iowa State University, Ames, Iowa). Retrieved from http://lib.dr.iastate.edu/etd/10624

Gonyea, R. M. (2008, February). *The impact of study abroad on senior year engagement*. Paper presented at the annual meeting of the Association for the Study of Higher Education, Jacksonville, FL.

Hopkins, J. R. (1999). Studying abroad as a form of experiential education. *Liberal Education, 85*(3), 36–41.

Ingraham, E. C., & Peterson, D. L. (2004). Assessing the impact of study abroad on student learning at Michigan State University. *Frontiers: The Interdisciplinary Journal of Study Abroad, 10*, pp. 83–100. Retrieved from https://doi.org/10.1080/14675980903370847

Kuh, G. D., & Schneider, C. G. (2008). *High impact educational practices: What they are, who as access to them, and why they matter.* Washington, DC: Association of American Colleges and Universities.

Malmgren, J., & Galvin, J. (2008). Effects of study abroad participation on student graduation rates: a study of three incoming freshman cohorts at the University of Minnesota, Twin Cities. *NACADA Journal, 28*(1), 29–42.

McLeod, M., & Wainwright, P. (2009). Researching the study abroad experience. *Journal of Studies in International Education, 13*(1), 66–71.

Murphy, D., Sahakyan, N., Yong-Yi, D., & Magnan, S. S. (2014). The impact of study abroad on the global engagement of university graduates. *Frontiers: The interdisciplinary journal of study abroad, 24*, 1–24.

Murphy-Lejeune, E. (2002). *Student mobility and narrative in Europe: The new strangers.* London: Routledge.

Paige, R. M., Fry, G. W., Stallman, E. M., Josić, J., & Jon, J.-E. (2009). Study abroad for global engagement: The long-term impact of mobility experiences. Intercutural Education, 20(supl 1), S29-S44.

Sutton, R. C., & Rubin, D. L. (2004). The GLOSSARI project: Initial findings from a system-wide research initiative on study abroad learning outcomes. *Frontiers: The Interdisciplinary Journal of Study Abroad, 10*, 65–82.

Whitman, W. (1855). *Leaves of grass.* Originally published 1855. ©2009 Sam Torode. Americanrenaissancebooks.com

Zhao, Y., Meyers, L., & Meyers, B. (2009). Cross-cultural immersion in China: Preparing pre-service elementary teachers to work with diverse student populations in the United States. *Asia-Pacific Journal of Teacher Education, 37*(3), 295–317.

Hope

I spend a great deal of time encouraging my pre-service teachers never to assume anything about children. The circumstances of their lives influence their behavior, success, or lack of success in the classroom. Unraveling the mysteries behind children's actions and implementing appropriate strategies for academic and social success are the true challenges of teaching. This lesson is not lost on my own assessment of my university students, who bring a variety of lived experiences and circumstances to my classroom. Smiles, cooperation, and compliance often mask deeper concerns and troubles. At times, however, even with keen perceptive skills and efforts, diligent observations and personal interactions often fail to recognize a troubled soul.

Often shy and hesitant to risk the study abroad undertaking, some teeter on the edge of withdrawing their participation. Unaware of their personal challenges, my interactions often do little to get at the heart of the matter and offer proper encouragement. Usually, it is not until we have returned to the states and I begin to review the submitted digital stories about their experiences, a requirement for the study abroad course, that my eyes are opened to their state of mind when they embarked on or during this adventure. Watching their YouTube videos and hearing their tales of hope and self-discovery not only open my eyes to what I didn't see coming, but, more importantly, warm my heart to know that the experience gave them the courage and determination to move forward and tackle personal issues. Research by Dolby (2004) found a significant restructuring of students' American identity as a result of their study abroad experiences, and Gemignani (2009) highlighted the result of students' introspection causing them to see themselves as more open with changes in perspectives. Their digital stories, complete with photos and appropriate Italian tunes, offer tales that brings tears to my eyes and remind me of why I have spent 44 years in the teaching profession. The essays which spoke to me of Hope echo the research showing the significance a study abroad experience plays in building self-confidence, promoting personal growth, and developing personal awareness (Braskamp, Braskamp, & Merrill, 2009; Clyne & Rizvi, 1998). For some there was one unrivaled experience that profoundly impacted the meaning of their experience (Gemignani 2009).

I chose to begin the book with the stories of Sarah and Emily. Theirs more than any of the others glowed with hope and personal awareness. I have shared their digital stories, which echo the narratives they submitted for the book, with faculty and potential study abroad students numerous times. I am proud to share with faculty authentic artifacts that testify to the richness of the study abroad experience we offer to our students, and I always sense a caught unawares feeling from potential students when the video messages are certainly something that they didn't see coming.

References

Braskamp, L. A., Braskamp, D. C., & Merrill, K. (2009). Assessing progress in global learning and development of students with education abroad experiences. *Frontiers: The Interdisciplinary Journal of Study Abroad, 18*, 101–118.

Clyne, F., & Rizvi, F. (1998). Outcomes of student exchange. In D. Davis & A. Olsen (Eds.), *Outcomes of international education* (pp. 35–49). Sydney: IDP Education Australia.

Dolby, N. (2004). Encountering an American self: Study abroad and national identity. {Electronic version}. *Comparative Education Review, 48(2)*, 150–173.

Gemignani, C. L. (2009). *Understanding the study abroad experience of university students.* (Graduate thesis dissertation, Iowa State University, Ames, Iowa). Retrieved from http://lib.dr.iastate.edu/etd/10624

CHAPTER ONE

An Opportunity to Run Away

SARAH ERDMAN[1]

I remember when all the colors started to fade. Life did not seem as bright. The blues of the sky seemed to dissolve into a lukewarm grey, the greens of the grass transformed into a muddy brown, and the brightness of life had dulled. It was that month when I experienced my first real loss. I was unsure of who I was, and how to move forward. It was then that my trip to Italy became my escape from reality. I thought of it as running away from my problems and running to a place and people who knew nothing about me. They would not ask me what I was feeling or how things were going. It was a fresh start, and I could not have been more excited.

When I received the information about my host family the month before I left for Modena, Italy, I initially wondered why I had been placed with my family. I was used to a nuclear household with two parents and an older brother, but my Italian host family consisted of a divorced mother and two little sisters. With the days counting down to my departure, I was more and more confused. How could these people like me when I did not even like myself? My life-long companions, Anxiety and Depression, pressured me to withdraw my participation in the program, but I knew I needed to go. Blindly, I stepped onto the airplane in May with a group of strangers and flew off to Italy.

The travel time to Modena seemed like forever, and I was already missing my family. During our layover in New York I remember reaching out to my boyfriend, telling him that I already felt far from home. I expressed my anxieties about leaving, afraid of the change and that my loved ones would forget me. With some words of wisdom and a leap of faith, I boarded the second leg of our flight to Italy, ready for the new adventure.

When I arrived in Modena, I immediately felt at home. Maybe it was the classic architecture, or that every Italian looked like they could be related to me. Something about the city and the attitude of the country made me feel at ease. My twenty years of battling anxiety and depression seemed to hit pause, and I felt myself breathe for the first time in months. Considering I was experiencing these feelings only on the bus ride to Modena from the airport in Milan, I was ready to meet my family. At first glance, stepping off the bus and into the arms of my host mother was overwhelming to say the least! I was immediately bombarded with hugs, kisses, and, "Are you cold?" We drove back to my new home for the month, where my host sisters, their father and grandmother greeted me. The combination of the new people, new environment, jet lag, and lack of sleep could have easily been enough to send me into a panic. However, this time things were different. While I missed my family back in Georgia, I knew something special was waiting for me this month.

Meeting my class was similar to meeting my family. At that point, I was used to feeling like a foreigner and I was soaking in every opportunity that I could to learn. My first challenge being abroad was, of course, the language barrier. The only situation where I felt like it was a problem was in the school and my Italian classroom, but I used it to my advantage. In the Italian schools, students will cycle through different teachers on a rotation, and only one of my two mentor teachers was comfortable speaking English. This meant that two out of my five days spent in the school were typically spent in a chair in the corner of the room, not talking to anyone. For the first few days, I sat in the corner when the non-English speaking teacher was in the room. She felt uncomfortable using broken English, so she instead decided to not talk to me or attempt to incorporate me with the class. Over time, I developed relationships with my students nonverbally. They realized I had no problem acting out different words and phrases, and our daily games of charades became my new routine. With my other teacher, who was comfortable speaking English, I taught the children different songs, games, and basic classroom vocabulary in English. Over time, I formed a bond with my student who was labeled as having an intellectual disability. I began to realize that this boy was very misunderstood. Teachers had not found ways to communicate with him, and he was always frustrated that he was not being understood. A part of me wants to think that he and I shared the same struggles in the school. No one could understand either of us for whatever reason, whether it was intellectual or lack of language, and it brought us together. I remember the first day he came over to me and played with my jewelry and then sat on my lap and played with my hands. We made a little language, just the two of us. He could see when I was getting tired, and I was able to figure out his different triggers and how to calm him. Slowly but surely, I became the girl who could understand the "complicated student," and he at last was visible.

This seemed to be the trend of the trip for me, being seen. It did not take long for me to discover why I was placed in my host family. It turns out my host mother is one of the most incredible people I have ever met. A survivor of breast cancer, she taught me what it means to be strong, to have courage, and to beat the odds. One night at dinner, she talked about her story. I learned the details of her life, what she was proud of and what she was not, and I did the same. For the first time, I told my secret. I told my host mother that I ran away to Italy to escape the pain in America. I disclosed the hurt in my heart, caused by loss. It was that night where she started to call me "her special daughter." From there, my role in my host family deepened. My two little sisters found ways to communicate with me. The older of the two was already fluent in English, so we became close almost immediately. We shared bad date stories, funny memories, and general advice. I had never been a big sister until this point, and I knew after this trip I would always be theirs. My younger sister was not comfortable with her English so for a while she used a translator app and showed me what she wanted to say. Things were very quiet between the two of us, but on our walks to school together every day we became more comfortable with each other. She would brag to her friends about her "American sister" who taught in the first grade hallway, and she started telling me about her days at school. Our big breakthrough happened at my host dad's house. With my host parents being recently divorced, I could tell my younger sister was having a hard time with the separation. The two of us sat on a swing outside and in our broken English I told her that things were going to be okay and that she was loved by her entire family—myself included. Later that evening while we played Jenga, my younger sister used the blocks to write "Ester loves Sarah", and I knew then that Modena was my home.

My relationships with the other American girls on the trip even changed. With the immersion experience, we all experienced feelings of loneliness from time to time, so we were always there to have each other's backs. I did not know any of the girls on my trip well, but as the weeks went on, I found my niche. I was able to relate to girls on the deepest of levels, and share laughs that I had not felt in months. The trip was orchestrated in a way where as soon as the immersion became overwhelming, it was time for a group trip for the American students. The program directors had a sixth sense for seeing around corners and knowing when to intervene in order to keep the group cohesive and to head off anxieties. They were incredibly supportive and knew exactly when to hold a hand or give a hug.

One day while I was getting a ride back to my host family's apartment with Roberta, a VLC co-owner, we talked about the experience and why I was matched with my family. Even though she had only seen a vague application from me, Roberta saw straight through me and was able to match me with the perfect hosts. I felt transparent. I told her why I was in Italy and what I was taking from the experience. It was the same with our university program director. She knew I was one of the youngest on the trip and I had little teaching experience, but she always managed to keep me calm and ensure that I was having a good time.

This trip changed me. During a day trip to Cinque Terre some friends and I decided to hike to the top of an island, a view we had all seen on computer desktops, postcards, and social media posts. It was a brutal hike in the middle of a hot day, and we all struggled to get to the top. With every step, I thought about what brought me to Italy, and the experiences that I never saw coming. I missed my home and my family back in the United States, but something about Modena made me feel at ease. When my foot hit the top of the hiking trail and I looked to see the view below me, I lost my breath. In front of me was the most spectacular scene. Most importantly, I felt color come back into my world. The shades of grey and muddled tones turned into vibrant hues, dancing in full vision. I was almost blinded by the image of the world in front of me. I felt myself fill with life, light, and warmth. Finally, I felt like me again. My legs may have ached, and the sweat may have dripped down my back, but that day I held my head so high I was always looking at the clouds.

My last day in Modena was excruciating. How could I possibly thank the people who helped me find myself? I spent the afternoon with my host mom, tasting Modena's sweet balsamic vinegar and doing some last minute shopping. We could hardly look at each other without tears filling our eyes. That evening I went to my sisters' dance recital. Sitting in the auditorium watching the dancers express themselves on stage filled my heart with joy. Tears streamed down my face as I gave the dancers a standing ovation, waiting to hug my sisters tight and never let them go. The rest of the night was filled with tears, extended hugs, and "see you laters." As I stepped into the car on the way to my bus, my younger sister gave me a package—a block from the Jenga set that she used to say she loved me. I held that block close, and I still keep it with me, ready to bring it back and complete our tower again. As our charter bus rolled away from Modena, my host mother pressed her hand against my window, tears streaming down her face. I placed my hand against hers, the glass separating us. Part of my heart was left in Modena that night. With my host mom, whose strong spirit keeps me going on my worst days. To my sister, whose passion for life reminds me to keep my hopes high. To my younger sister, whose unselfishness encourages me to spread kindness everywhere I go. To my host dad, who showed me his love of cuisine, wine, and music. To Modena, the place that saved my life.

My month as a foreign exchange student taught me many things. I learned to really laugh. The kind that makes your stomach hurt and your eyes fill with tears.

I learned to not take things so seriously and to be spontaneous. I learned how to love the world, the people around me, and most importantly, myself. My hope was restored. To the city of Modena and mi familigia, it wasn't goodbye. It was "a presto"—see you later.

Note

1. Sarah Erdman, B.S.Ed., Early Childhood Education Graduate, University of Georgia.

CHAPTER TWO

Packing and Unpacking

EMILY GWALTNEY[1]

"A mind that is stretched by a new experience can never go back to its old dimensions."
—OLIVER WENDELL HOLMES

During the spring of 2016, I had the opportunity to study abroad for a few months. Little did I know that it would change my whole life. I left Atlanta and flew to Modena, Italy with a large group of girls that thrived and struggled as a team. These girls completely enriched my experience, but I left my heart with another group of people—my Italian host family. I stepped onto Italian soil and gained another set of parents and four new siblings (one set of triplet boys and their younger sister). They welcomed me with open arms into their family and into their home. This family was my support system and my refuge during the program. Whatever instability or challenge I faced during the day, whether it was a long day at school or a six-hour stay in an Italian emergency room, I knew I was coming home to my family and that was my favorite part of every day. As much as they loved on me and cheered me on, staying in their home and spending time in their country made me realize something monumental—I would rather have experiences than things.

I would rather spend the money I have going places with people that I love than having the newest clothes or living extravagantly. I realized while in Italy that I did not need a lot of material things. I brought many things with me that I thought I would need, and it turns out that I never even took them out of my suitcase. My host family lived well, but I could tell quite easily what they valued and what they considered a luxury. I spent many memorable moments with my host brothers, exploring places that none of us had been before. And these small and often loud moments are what I treasure most about my trip.

Once shy and reluctant to take chances, I embraced the opportunities for getting lost. I relied solely on a foldout map in Venice and wandered around with little direction in Verona. These were wonderful, freeing opportunities to soak in the geography of unfamiliar places and to rely on my foundational sense of direction to get me back to where I needed to be. Without the use of Google Maps and iPhone resources, I relied on memory and senses—that street corner with the postcard seller and the Zara store across the street. I embraced getting lost in Italy and absorbing what the Italian environment has to offer. In every direction there were beautiful people and breathtaking scenery.

My study abroad experience did not stop when the program ended. I stayed on in Modena as a counselor in an English summer camp for two weeks, teaching and loving on Italian students and then spent another month with my own Italian grandparents in Perugia. With my grandparents I traveled across the country and saw some of the most breathtaking places on Earth. I did not have access to all of the things that I am used to at home, so it was an adjustment. However, how could I have a bad attitude when I was travelling and spending time in a country that is so close to my heart? I pushed every negative feeling out, and what was left was complete and utter gratitude for everything I had seen and experienced on my two-month journey.

Living out of suitcases forced me to prioritize and throw out things that I did not need. Changed by all that I had seen, experienced, and absorbed during my two- month adventure, I returned home to the states and began the process of uncluttering my life. This was one of the first things on my to-do list. I think this new minimalistic mindset will last a lifetime. With my renewed priorities, I felt my relationships growing deeper, similar to the ones in the country that stole my heart in only a few short weeks.

My time in Italy seemed like it would last forever, but it went by in the blink of an eye. Honestly, this trip rocked me to my core. It certainly knocked me off my American high horse and taught me what I truly value. Relationships were built over loud breakfasts of coffee and playing Monopoly with my precious host siblings. Relationships were built struggling to communicate about swamp animals in my third-grade class at San Geminiano Elementary School and sitting in an emergency room waiting area when I thought I had broken a rib from coughing incessantly for five weeks straight. They were built learning camp songs and trekking through historic cities where the greats walked before us. They were built witnessing my beautiful little host sister perform in her ballet recital. The grace and poise with which she moved brought me to a completely new level of appreciation for her. Honestly, I did not even know that I liked ballet before I watched her dance. I am grateful to her for that, for teaching me something about myself I did not know and for sharing what she loves with me. My experiences in Italy reinforced the value of people and my relationships with them. The study abroad program to Modena provided me with a multitude of learning experiences and memories that I never saw coming. I learned how well I can "adult" when thrown into an Italian airport flying by myself for the first time. I learned to fit an impossible number of pictures onto my phone. I learned to speak Italian from listening to the squeaky voices of third graders. I learned to fit an entire pizza, and then gelato, into my stomach. I learned to genuinely appreciate art. I learned how to explain America to someone who has never been there. I learned how to listen carefully and speak slowly when navigating a strange language. I learned that I was more grown up at the end of the experience than at the beginning, and that was frightening.

Italy gave me genuine friends that I will hold close for the rest of my life. It united me with family members that I had never met, and introduced me to an incredible host family—people that I will consider my family from now on. It gave me a burning desire to travel. It gave me courage to try new things. It gave me a confidence that I did not have when I arrived in the country. It gave me insight into my plans. It gave me too much food. It gave me patience and boldness, and it gave me a new outlook on life. It gave me incredible opportunities that pushed me out of my comfort zone. It gave me hope for the future. For all of these things I am thankful.

Note

1. Emily Gwaltney, Early Childhood Education Teacher Candidate, University of Georgia.

PART TWO

Discovery

Assuming the mindset that the UGA/Modena Schools Study Abroad Program is purely an educational opportunity can limit the imagination and focus. It can give pause to even considering participation and what such an experience can offer. The merits of involvement are questioned. For many who take the plunge and choose to participate in such a venture they enter into it with a sense of tunnel vision. Presumptions, doubts, worries, and limited travel experience cloud their vision and give rise to many questions. What can Italian children gain from this experience? How can I possibly learn from those who do not speak my language? How authentic can this teaching opportunity really be? Negativity creeps in and they can only perceive the half-empty glass. Their thoughts are more concerned with what certainly cannot be instead of what can. The only thing they are confident about is the certainty that it will be easy to leave once the program ends. Yet, out of all their expectations and presumptions, the reality of this notion is undeniably something that they didn't see coming. "You will want to see family and friends from home but you won't want to leave the life you made abroad. You will miss having café con leche every day. You will miss your corner bakery. You will miss the beautiful architecture. If there's one reality you will experience, however, it is that you will want to come back" (Benson, 2016, p. 1).

It is perhaps those with this mindset who are most astounded by what they did not see coming. Convinced of what is surely to be a limited, confusing, and awkward experience, they are the most amazed by the unexpected discoveries. Their imaginations are expanded. They suddenly view the world with different lenses. Possibilities become realities, and an eagerness to explore and discover even more dismisses their once doubtful and negative thoughts.

It would be easy to chide these participants with "I told you so" or "if you had only listened" remarks. However, the astounding changes of heart and attitude are gratifying and uplifting and dissolve any desires to prove a point in an admonishing manner or tone. In a sense, their change of spirit is often something I did not see coming. As Hopkins (1999) asserts, experiential learning opportunities, such as studying abroad, force students to look inward and outward. Finding themselves in a new cultural context, they must deal with their views of self and their cultural assumptions, and in so doing experience dramatic self-development. Dwyer (2004) emphasizes that those participating in cross-cultural experiences have a better sense of their own cultural values and biases and acquire a more sophisticated way of looking at the world. Participants are left with new thoughts, ideas, and an eagerness to share with family and friends (Malicki & Potts, 2013).

These ideas certainly reverberate in the Discovery narratives. Kelli, Zarina, Benedetta, Tatyana, Gloria and Shelly have very different stories to share. Yet, each discovered something during the experience. Representing a multicultural pool of their own, they highlight the commonalities that exist between them brought about by their shared experiences. They were eager to reveal what they discovered.

References

Benson, A. (2016). *Study abroad expectations vs. reality: A student's reflection.* Available from http://bcastudyabroad.org/blog/2016/12/study-abroad-expectations-vs-reality-a-students-reflection

Dwyer, M. M. (2004). More is better: The impact of study abroad program duration. *Frontiers: The Interdisciplinary Journal of Study Abroad, 10*, 151–163.

Hopkins, J. R. (1999). Studying abroad as a form of experiential education. *Liberal Education, 85*(3), 36–45.

Malicki, R., & Potts, D. (2013). *The outcomes of outbound student mobility. A summary of academic literature.* Retrieved from http://aimoverseas.com.au/wp-content/uploads/2013/08/UAAsiaBoundOutcomesResearch-Final.pdf

CHAPTER THREE

That Needed Push

KELLI LEWIS DANIELS[1]

At the age of 22, I found myself intrigued with the idea of studying in Italy and wanting to experience all it had to offer. Yet, because of the unknown, I could not decide if it would all be worth it in the end. A former professor who had pushed and challenged me like no other, once again saw something in me that I did not see in myself and suggested I be a part of the UGA/Modena Schools Study Abroad Program in Modena, Italy. Participation presented the opportunity for travel and adventure while earning credit towards my masters of education degree in early childhood education. I had heard of studying abroad but never thought it was for me, and I gave her a list of reasons why. I did not consider myself the outgoing and adventurous type, and I was not too fond of the idea of being thousands of miles away from my family for almost an entire month! I would turn another year older three days after arriving in Modena, so I would miss celebrating my special day and Mother's Day with my family. The thought of living with a family I had never met who spoke limited English gave me lots of anxiety. Dr. Tolley kept pushing. I kept finding excuses, none of which was plausible in her opinion. With a leap of faith, I agreed to participate. This was the hardest thing I had ever done! On May 2nd, five days before leaving for the trip, I started a journal. On day one, I wrote, "I have no idea what to expect, and I think that is the worst part about it. I am excited to see what God has in store for me, and all I will experience. I know I will come back a much stronger person." These words turned out to be so true! On May 8th,

I was on a plane to Italy and there was no turning back! There was so much that I did not see coming.

On one of the first days in my new surroundings I blew a fuse in my host family's house trying to use my hair straightener. Nobody was home, and I barely knew what to do in such a situation in my own apartment back in America, much less in a stranger's home in another country! This was sure to be interesting! I later told my host parents, mostly communicating with movements and acting out the scenario. I was quickly finding out what it must feel like for those who come to America and speak little or no English.

I was assigned to Galilei Elementary School, and my first day visiting my second grade classroom was my birthday. They were so sweet and made me feel so special! The students all sang Happy Birthday to me in English, and they had prepared an assortment of snacks for celebrating. Although I understood very little of what they were saying, communicating was easier than I anticipated because of their expressive faces. I spent most of the time feeling lost, but I soaked up every moment. I often felt as if I were deaf and had to solely depend on facial expressions and body language. During math class, however, it was much easier to figure out what was going on because numbers are universal. I could walk around the room and help by looking at the student's work and say "si" or "no." Nonetheless, as the days went on, it was very frustrating to not be able to communicate with the teachers and students. I desperately wanted to have actual conversations with them. I kept thinking to myself that I must remember these feelings. This experience provided a glimpse of what it must be like for immigrant students who may find themselves in my future classroom knowing little or no English. The difficulty and frightening feeling of trying to fit in, make friends, and learn all at the same time would be overwhelming. Here I was, an adult, knowing my time confronted by this language barrier was limited. I quickly empathized with immigrant children moving to America with family and realized how frightening this must be.

My host family made me feel very special on my birthday, as well! They discovered that my best friend and roommate in America was also on the study abroad trip and invited her to dinner at their house. We ate a big dinner as we did most nights while in Italy. We had pasta, rice, asparagus, peas, hamburger patties, and fried potatoes. They also prepared a delicious cake with fruit on top. We played games, and my two host brothers put the game in English. They were so thoughtful and kind! I did not know my friend was coming that day. It was a nice surprise. Most of the entire stay in Italy was a surprise. I rarely knew what was going on, where we were going, or what to prepare for. This was not necessarily easy for a person who planned EVERYTHING and was not very spontaneous. I learned to live more in the moment rather than worrying about the future. This newly found sense of spontaneity also taught me to not be afraid of going with the flow sometimes and that it is okay if things do not work out as planned. I continue to struggle with this but I have to say that spending that month in Italy made me realize this much more clearly than in my experiences in America and in my own familiar surroundings.

The weather consisted of rain … a lot! It was frustrating at times, because I spent a lot of time outside, getting from one place to another. However, that was just all part of the experience. Italians are not dependent on vehicles nearly as much as Americans. They have a different culture and way of living. Most families have one car. Many rely on bikes or the public bus system, one of the many differences that I noticed between Italian and American cultures. I found Italians to be much more simplistic and frugal; they need very little to make them happy, contrary to the materialistic ways of Americans. It was nice and comforting to see such a loving culture that was perfectly fine and content with having less of the material things.

In my classroom there was one little boy who touched my heart in a very special way. His name was Pascal and he really took to me quickly. He was very loving and always happy to see me. There was a woman who came to get him each day at school for a short period of time. I kind of thought she was perhaps a counselor or held a similar type of position. She told me that Pascal's mother lived in Germany and he missed her very much. My heart broke for him and the fact that he lived so far away from his mother. I quickly realized that language was not necessary for understanding Pascal's sadness and sense of loss. I took many opportunities to work with him and show him kindness in hopes of alleviating some of his sadness.

My favorite days with my class were when I taught a lesson. It was a challenge to teach without language, but through lots of patience, it all worked out! I chose to do a math lesson and create a bar graph. I asked the students to name their favorite vegetable. The students were to draw the vegetable and write it in English on a sticky note then come to the board and place the note on the graph to create bars. We discussed the chart together and discovered that carrots were the favorite class vegetable. We played Hot Potato and the teacher wrote "bollente patata" on the board for the class to see the name of the game in Italian. The students absolutely loved learning the new game and playing it together. I was so thankful for the time that I was able to share with them. I thought about how cool it would have been to have an Italian college student visit my classroom when I was in second grade! I want to think that memory is something those students will always keep and maybe some will even be inspired to travel to distant places when they are older. I suddenly became aware of the possible lasting impressions of my being a part of their class and lives, even if only for a short time.

The Italian food was delicious, and six years later, I can still remember the distinct flavors and smells. The restaurants we visited on our excursions were good, but the foods made in the home of my host family were the best. It is difficult to choose a favorite because there was something special about them all. "Pasta Ragu" was one of my favorite meals. It seems to be what we call spaghetti … noodles, red sauce, and meat. There was something different, though, that made it taste much more authentic. I watched my host mom make it several times, making notes as best I could, but I have yet to replicate the taste and flavor that I found in hers.

This experience taught me more than I can ever put into words. It made me a better teacher and a better person. It was a worthwhile investment, but I would be lying if I said it was easy. Living in unfamiliar settings with complete strangers, hearing almost no English spoken, and learning how to survive through newly found ways of communication was very challenging, nerve-wracking, exciting, frustrating, and wonderful all at the same time. I keep a photograph of myself with my host family in my classroom as a reminder of the precious memories and all that I learned about life and about myself. Each year my new group of American third graders asks me who those people are, and I am able to share with them this part of my life and describe to them my second-grade classroom in another country. I have had new students come and go from my classroom. My Italian experience has given me the encouragement, support, confidence, and understanding needed to fulfill these students' needs in ways that I did not have before. I am forever changed because of this wonderful opportunity—the surprise I never saw coming.

Note

1. Kelli Lewis Daniels, 3rd Grade Teacher, The Academy for Classical Education.

CHAPTER FOUR

The White Rose

ZARINA MAUDE WAFULA[1]

I have been in multiple airports in my life. Traveling between America and Kenya always requires a plane ride. I grew up in Kenya as a good Catholic family girl. I had a successful banking career and dropped all of it to come to America to study to be a teacher. My travels and ambitions have, at times, made me nervous about new people and new experiences, but for some reason, stepping off that plane in Italy made butterflies explode in my stomach. Would my host family actually enjoy living with me? Could I adjust to another new culture? Would I do well teaching in a new school? Would I be respected?

The journey to my study abroad program was different from any of my compatriots. I am the only non-American to participate in this program to date, and it is my hope that my story will encourage other students like me to study abroad. My interest in the study abroad program started about a year or more before I landed in Milan with the group. I was doubtful that I could participate in a USA exchange program due to visa concerns, money concerns, and just about everything else concerns. There were additional preliminaries pertinent to my participation, such as a trip to Miami to secure the proper visa.

Once this was accomplished, I was still searching for ways to finance the trip. Out of the blue, an American friend who considers me his adopted daughter offered to pay the program fee. This gesture is one of the many acts of generosity that Americans have bestowed on me during my studies in the United States. Now fully committed to the program, I began to prepare myself for yet another culture shock, but I looked forward to comparing and contrasting cultures. The program in Italy offered me the opportunity to understand and compare three different cultures and three different styles of teaching. I came away with the understanding that while cultures can differ drastically, people and especially children, are universal, and we have much more in common that we think.

I was first introduced to my Italian host family via a letter from my host mom detailing important aspects of the family that she thought I should know before my travels. I immediately like them. Giuliani and Marcelo were a typical Italian couple with three young girls, two of whom were five-year-old twins. Despite our early and frequent email exchanges, I was still nervous to meet them. I was going to be placed into a full and functioning family and was expected to be part of it. For an entire month, I would be Zarina Wafula part of the Sachetti family, which ended up being one of the highlights of my life. UGA and Victoria Language and Culture were instrumental in ensuring that both my stay and travels went smoothly. The teachers and students at Calvino school were phenomenal and supportive in facilitating my educational experience, and last but not least, my steady family made me feel at home and welcomed as their daughter. Many are the days we stayed up late in the night talking about everything and nothing. The kids made me laugh a lot with their infectious laughter and mischiefs with the cat. The nanny, Auror, gave me hope that it is possible to know or learn a new language and be fluent. I found that everyone I met was warm and welcoming.

Arriving from the airport on that first day I scanned the crowd for a set of twins, expecting the whole family of five to meet me there. However, only Giuliana and Cecilia were waiting for me. Immediately, Cecilia started chattering to me, and I realized how I had missed living with little ones. I knew my stay would be beautiful and amazing when I saw Giuliana with her dark, cropped hair smiling at me. Cecilia was the spitting image of her mother with an amazing warm, impish grin that won me over in less than a second. Cecilia was aware that I speak Swahili, and she asked me how to say white rose in Swahili? "Rosi nyeupe," I answered and smiled at her and her interesting question. It was the Sachetti family children, Livia, Ottavia, and Cecilia, that reminded me that children are children, whether American, Kenyan, or Italian.

Later I found myself reflecting on Cecilia's question and was reminded of a truism. Often we find ourselves missing some aspect of our life or culture that at times we consider annoying. Kenyan extended families are very close, and I was frequently around my nieces and nephews. I was often annoyed with them when they invaded my space, went through my packages and luggage, or hit me with a myriad of questions. Being in Italy away from them, I found that I missed that element of my life. It was nostalgic. Cecilia's random question reminded me of my nieces and nephews and exposed me to her childhood innocence, creativity, and curiosity that I love so much about children. I loved the constant questions from the Sachetti girls. I missed that element of my home culture and family, so living with these three little girls brought me back home.

Shortly after arriving at the home of my host family, the girls eagerly began to unpack my suitcases and inspect every item. Marcelo and Giuliana seemed horrified and tried to shoot the girls away from my luggage, but I was very happy to indulge them. Many hands make light work. Plus, I knew that they were looking for the gifts I had promised them. I quickly brought out books and jewelry—books in English from America, books from my home continent of Africa, and beaded jewelry. The girls were thrilled with their gifts. They immediately asked me to read the storybooks while they rubbed the beads with their fingers. Never once did I feel like a stranger in my new Italian home.

My first few days in Italy were a whirlwind of activity. The family was very active, and soon I joined the routines of walking with them to pick up the children, meeting friends for dinner, and learning about Italian culture. I quickly learned universal lessons—family is important, and children fight with each other in all families. I attended mass with Giuliana and was surprised to see that it was conducted in Latin. I recognized the rhythm of responsive readings, the familiar melodies, the homily from the priest, and the scripture readings that are universal. I was reminded of home and provided with a great sense of peace for the next month.

My Italian experience led to many personal discoveries after touring different Italian cities and experiencing firsthand what I had only seen and read in books. I acquired a love of history. I was reminded of how small the world really is when Giuliana served me tea from my native Kenya, a personal favorite of hers, as well. I adopted the philosophy of expecting new places to be different and to embrace those differences and learn from them. My placement in the middle school gave me a deeper understanding of adolescence, and I gained confidence and comfort in teaching older children. I learned from daily interactions with the students and their teachers that generosity is a cornerstone of Italian hospitality. I was educated to the many types of pasta and was reminded of my African roots when introduced to polenta. I now considered a third continent a place to call home and recognized the connections and bonds that I so easily formed in such a short amount of time.

I still keep in touch with my Italian family and love knowing that there are people around the world that care about me. I hope to return to Italy and see how those beautiful little girls have grown. I have an open invitation from the family. They, too, have an open invitation to visit me whether in America or Kenya. The girls are looking forward to visiting the rift valley in Kenya. My own mom is looking forward to hosting the family having had a chance to talk with Giuliana and connecting like long lost friends. What I learned in Italy was far more than book knowledge, and I hope my words convey how the trip impacted my life.

Note

1. Zarina Maude Wafula, Teacher, Woodland Star International School (Kenya).

CHAPTER FIVE

The Need for the "Other"

BENEDETTA PANTOLI[1]

When I first met Roberto from Victoria Language and Culture, who proposed to our Modena Municipality an opportunity to host a group of American students for a one month internship in our preschools and kindergartens, I must admit I was very worried. Schools are places of hospitality, but hosting for a month young foreign students who speak only English, and, in addition to that, have them teach children aged 3 to 5, seemed a bit risky to me. I questioned how we would integrate the students into our educational days, what kind of relationships they could possibly create with the children and the teachers in such a short amount of time, and what significance they could make in their own everyday lives, both in schools and out. In those initial conversations with Roberta she offered powerful and meaningful opportunities—rich experiences that I didn't see coming. It has been such a long time since that first meeting and now, each year, I cannot wait for our American students to arrive.

The entire process, starting from exchanging emails with the girls to the time when they actually arrive in our schools and interact with our children, revealed great opportunities for both our children and our teachers. In our schools, where English is proposed from the age of 3, this American study abroad program integrating language education promotes our core belief that learning takes place when there is an interaction between the student and the "others"—that is, someone who does not speak our language and uses his own language to build up relationships and interact with other people.

Children actively build up their own knowledge. Experience is essential for the child's learning process. It is in this way of getting into direct contact, seeing firsthand, acting, asking questions that he can develop his own curiosity and his ideas about the world. By interacting with the others, the child finds room for new elaborations to mediate his own point of view. Children are surprised when they encounter a different language, they approach it with a curiosity, with a variety of different sounds, and elaborate hypotheses on how the said language works, and explore many attempts at expressing themselves. They listen to it and focus on what captures their curiosity. That is why this study abroad cultural exchange program is so important from a teaching/learning point of view, because it gives the children the possibility to experience the other on a daily basis.

In addition, the hosting experience allows us to rediscover our daily life, to give a new meaning to its customs and traditions and to get to know new perspectives through opening up to other cultures. For these reasons, every year, I wait for the new students as an indispensable opportunity for cultural and human growth for both our children and our educational services.

Note

1.   Benedetta Pantoli, Chief Officer, Modena Municipality Schools and Education Services.

CHAPTER SIX

Figuring Out the Puzzle

TATYANNA VINCENTY[1]

Italy was like a puzzle, a beautiful puzzle, and the thousands of pieces were difficult to put together. The edges of the puzzle were laid out nicely in pre-departure meetings. I knew our calendar, the other thirty-one girls on the trip, what to bring, what to leave, and a few Italian phrases. I had even started corresponding with my host family in the weeks before I left the states. I had all the edges of the puzzle pieced together and was excited to see the rest of the pieces fall easily into place. However, I was soon to discover that the puzzle was not to come together as easily as I anticipated.

Some pieces fell into place exactly as I had planned. The food was delicious, my host family was incredible, and the sights were breathtaking. However, these beautiful sights and the urge to not miss a single one turned into my first unexpected challenge. After landing at the airport in Milan, all of the girls slept during the three-hour bus ride to Modena. I, however, refused to sleep and opted, instead, to take in the scenery along the way. What I never anticipated was once I arrived in Modena and was safely swept away by my host family, I would sleep for the next seventeen hours. I lost an entire day. Opportunities to continue working on my Italian puzzle were lost. While everyone else was at church, or soccer games, or meeting other family members, I was asleep. I even caused my host sister to miss her friends christening, because she was actually waiting for me to wake up. I felt terrible.

As the days passed I shortsightedly began to compare my experiences with those of others on the trip, thinking I was somehow missing experiences and, therefore, failing to gather the pieces to my puzzle. I did not sample cannoli. I did not have an opportunity to go to Rome. I did not have a huge host family like I expected. For a while, I thought I was missing out. In reality, I was not appreciating what was right in front of me. I was served pasta and bread, two of my favorite foods, every single day. I discovered that French fries are my favorite pizza topping. Why hasn't America caught on to this? Sure, I did not get the opportunity to go to Rome like Lizzie Maguire and meet Paulo, but the memories that I made in Florence and Venice are far more meaningful than any coin I could have thrown in a fountain. And although there were only two Rinaldis, Euge had the energy of all three of my own American siblings combined.

Some aspects of my trip did not go as planned. It even ended a bit more bitter than sweet. It was at this time that I realized that the picture of Italy that I had imagined on the puzzle box was not the puzzle that was meant for me to piece together. I finally understood that I was not missing necessary puzzle pieces. I was simply picturing the wrong puzzle. I was so caught up in making the experience fit the image of my perceived puzzle that I almost missed the puzzle that was meant for me to enjoy. I was a bit disappointed that I could not remain with my host family until the end of the program due to unavoidable circumstances. This was an authentic lesson in how unexpected events occur in all families and that adaptability is a universal message. However, looking back on the collection of pictures that were taken and the memories that were made, I realize that my Italian adventure was exactly what it was supposed to be, and I wouldn't trade it for the world. I am more than happy that Italy is now part of my personal puzzle collection.

Note

1. Tatyanna Vincenty, 2nd Grade Teacher, Cobb County (Georgia) School System.

CHAPTER SEVEN

One Month of Glory

HA-YOUNG (GLORIA) YU[1]

Though two years have passed, I often catch myself reminiscing about my time in Modena. It really was the most wonderful month. Reveling in the midst of a different culture, the greatest insight I gained was about the enduring nature of relationships.

Going on a study abroad trip was on my bucket list of things to do during college, so it did not take much mustering of courage in deciding to go to a foreign country. I found myself as a junior in college that the plethora of friends I made during my freshman year had dwindled down to just a handful. This became the norm, and making new friends often took me out of my comfort zone. The most nerve-wracking part of going abroad was that I would be living with a host family. Will my host family like me? Will my limited Italian suffice? Being an average amicable person, I reassured myself that I would get along just fine engaging in probable shallow and difficult to understand conversations.

The layover in Paris, landing in Bologna, and arriving in Modena was supposed to be a rather long journey, but all of a sudden, we were getting off the bus to meet our host families. I found myself already thinking that time was moving too fast.

As my host dad and I were headed home, I noticed a small Totoro keychain on his rearview mirror. My host family happened to be a Miyazaki fan like me! I, being Korean American, thought I was as different as can be from my Italian host family. So, that small keychain gave me great comfort knowing we had something in common, and reminded me of how small our world really is.

I had a big host family that consisted of Beppe, Lisa, Michi (brother 2), Benni, and Frenci. While the other host families had younger children, my siblings were mostly around my age. As soon as I arrived at their house, I was invited to go to an outdoor festival called Costaoila on the Rock. Though I was severely jetlagged, I tagged along. That first night there were few opportunities to marvel at the fact that I was in Italy, because my host brother introduced me to almost everyone we met on the street as his American sister. I was so thankful because they made me feel like a part of the family as soon as I met them.

I remember my cheeks hurting that night because I was smiling and laughing constantly. Though I was with people I met for the first time, including my "cousin" who lived on the floor beneath us in the apartment building, it was comfortable and fun in its own way. My host brother and new friends were thoughtful in explaining what everything was, especially about the food. The first night I had Modena's special fritto misto—an assortment of meats and cheeses produced in the area and served with the most amazing bread. I couldn't help but wonder what other adventures and delectable foods awaited.

One of my happiest moments in Modena was when the whole study abroad group was heading towards Piazza Grande. As we neared the restaurant I ran into my host cousin who was getting out of class. I excitedly greeted her and rejoined the group. At that moment Dr. Tolley remarked that I was already a local! That was probably the best compliment anyone could have given me. I felt proud and happy that I was becoming well-adjusted to this new city. I glamorized Italy so much that I could not fathom how people lived on a daily basis. This glamorous perception soon gave way to a more realistic one as I lived life with my host family. I was witness to sibling rivalries and the international inclination of parents to embarrass their children.

My host family had a lively pet bird named Leo. During one dinner, my oldest host brother, Michele, got up to give Leo some food. Michele had some trouble because Leo would not get away from the food bowl. Michele made several attempts to change out Leo's food bowl jumping back every time Leo got close to Michele's hand. After some time Michele came back to the dinner table and my host dad commented, "We have a Steve Irwin over here!" Beppe seriously had the best sense of humor.

Beppe also cooked a lot. All of his food was very tasty! My favorite was the pesto risotto and quail egg pastries. Towards the end of the trip, Beppe told me that while I stayed with them, I ate undercooked pasta three times! The way he told me made it sound like this was some sort of travesty. I hardly noticed and was simply thankful that he cared to notice.

I spent the last weekend in Milan where my host family took me around the city, and we explored the 2015 Food EXPO. Being in a tourist city, I felt special to be shown the sights by my host family. There were hordes of tourists following one guide, and I was thrilled at how much better and more authentic my experience was. I felt like a local as we shopped around and drank espresso at the bar.

At the EXPO there were countries from all over the world representing their national foods and sustainability ideas. My host family suggested that we try the food at the Korean Pavilion. I was amazed and appreciative that they would take an interest in my culture and me. I realized that they were not just serving as polite hosts during my stay in their home and in their country. They had an authentic and keen interest in knowing and understanding my Korean culture and me. It was such fun explaining each food and seeing them try everything. They seemed to enjoy it!

Saying goodbye was bittersweet. The day before I left we celebrated my youngest host brother's birthday and mine. Our birthdays were three days apart! Though they were occupied with Frenci's party, my host family still took time to celebrate my birthday with cakes and presents. There could not have been a better ending to my time in Modena.

My tech savvy host dad came up with a hashtag #OneMonthofGlory to commemorate my stay. I understood a little of how difficult it was for a family to accommodate a new person for a whole month, but they did it so well and with such hospitality. My host sister, who became like a real sister to me, promised to attend my wedding and I hers. Lisa, who I really depended on like a mom, had the most caring heart and kindest eyes.

The highlight of my study abroad experience was my host family. This aspect stands out among all the rest of my experiences during the month-long adventure. Though two years have passed I am still in communication with these wonderful people. The relationship formed with my host family has endured. Because of this, I have made lifelong friends and have a reason to return.

Note

1. Ha-Young (Gloria) Yu, Master of Arts in Teaching Candidate, University of Georgia.

CHAPTER EIGHT

Once Is Not Enough

SHELLY GLEATON BLAIR[1]

Prior to my study abroad trip to Modena Italy I was worried about living with a host family. I was a non-traditional student, a nearly 25 year old graduate student, half a decade older than most of the participants, who had been living on my own for four years. I grew up as basically an only child since my three siblings are 17–25 years older than me, so I had never shared a home and parents with other children. Also, my thoughts and anticipations were colored by my experiences from a study abroad trip to Spain five years earlier. That experience involved living in dormitories limiting cultural immersion—much different from what the Modena experience promised.

Needless to say, I was a bit nervous about living with a family again – much less a family of strangers, possibly young children, in an unfamiliar country and culture, speaking a language completely unknown to me. A bit of anxiety disappeared when I discovered that my siblings were in their teens and early twenties! Cecilia was 17 and Francesco was 22. With this new knowledge I began envisioning becoming friends with my host siblings rather than seeing my role as that of helper or mentor.

Upon arrival in Modena, the busload of students pulled into the parking lot where we were to meet the Italian families we would live with for the next few weeks. Admittedly, I was very worried about living with a strange family and suddenly having rules again after years of living on my own. Once I hopped off the bus and met my smiling host mother, Anna, and goofing-around host father, Fabrizio, my worries vanished! In the little Fiat, on the way to my new home for the next few weeks, Anna first said, "I am sorry, I do not speak very well English" so my nervousness inched its way back, but then I realized I didn't even know how to tell them, I don't speak Italian at all! I determined my language deficit was far greater than theirs. After a short time in the car they were warming up and talking to me some in English, as well as speaking amongst themselves in Italian. I was in the backseat desperately trying to figure out what they were saying to one another in Italian and smiling at my "new normal."

Once we made it to the house, my family showed me to my room on the third floor of their home. Their hospitality was overwhelming! My room had an awesome set up with a bedroom, balcony, and bathroom complete with a robe, towels, and small toiletries set out for me. These little gestures made me feel so welcomed in their family, and they were so thoughtful in their preparation for my arrival. I learned later from talking with other students that I had hit the lottery with my accommodations.

After unpacking and a family lunch, my host mother planned a bike trip into the city center with one of my classmates, Claire, and her host family. It is important to add that I had not ridden a bike since I was around 8 years old, so it was a bit of a challenge to make it from Amendola to Piazza della Pomposa, dodging traffic, road signs, poles, and pedestrians. The entire ride I was contemplating turning my phone off airplane mode so I could call for a taxi capable of hauling me and my bike back to my new house to avoid the ride back. Cost would be no consideration! We enjoyed gelato at Gelateria Pomposa and had a chance to unwind walking around and touring Modena's city center. We ambled along on the cobblestones taking in the sights, taking photos, and visiting some prominent places in the city center including Piazza Della Pomposa, the Duomo di Modena, Piazza Grande, and more. Once I successfully biked myself the few miles back home, we gathered for dinner and I met Anna's father, Nonno, who lives at the same house as my family in his own apartment. I struggled through telling him Ciao, piacere (hello, I am pleased to meet you), although I would be interested to know what I actually said to him.

On my first full day in Modena my host mother, Anna, took me on a walk to see the school where I would be working and to look around our neighborhood and the park nearby, Parco Giovanni Amendola. Later that afternoon, we went to the nearby town, Formigine, with Claire and her family. Being able to visit another town and tour the castle with local families made me feel more at-home with my new family because we were both experiencing something unfamiliar at the same time. Claire's family later drove Claire and me through the hills of Emilia

Romagna to see Castello di Montecuccolo and to our first restaurant experience in Italy, the Trattoria Valle, where we were introduced to tigelle and lardo for the first time!

After spending the first weekend immersed in the Italian culture with our host families, we joined our group for a class and a tour of Modena. We had lunch at Caffee Concerto in Piazza Grande and were able to try many local Italian dishes. Later we toured Modena and visited its historical city hall. The highlight of our time there was meeting Modena's Mayor, Giorgio Pighi, and later having an article in the paper spotlighting his welcome to our UGA group. We ended our tour by with a visit to Pasticceria Remondini where we met our good friend, Giulio, whom I would spend many days and evenings with over the next month (and the following two summers).

Our group was able to really get to know one another our first full week in Italy by touring Modena, Reggio Children, the MoMo, and Nido Forghieri. It was also so nice to have a built in time to discuss our experiences with one another, be able to talk to one another (in English!), and enjoy each other's company during our pizza nights.

When I first arrived at my school, I met Maria and Cinzia, my two host/mentor teachers in the cinque anni (5-year-olds) class. I was nervous and I could tell they were, too, although they did not speak any English and I did not speak any Italian. There was only one English-speaking teacher at my school and she only came on Wednesdays, so we created our own system for communication. We used a great deal of hand motions, similar to playing charades, to communicate with one another. We also scribbled tiny drawings to get our point across and frequently referred to my English/Italian dictionary when words were simply too complex or difficult to describe to one another. The children warmed up to me quickly, and by the second day they were drawing pictures for me, writing me notes, drawing to communicate with me and even referencing the dictionary (mind you, they were five years old, so they often could not find the word they were looking for and had to ask one of their teachers for assistance).

The day before my first day of school, my host family took me to the Modena Mall to see some of the local shops and grocery store. Later that evening, we went to the Teatro Communale Luciano Pavarotti (Pavarotti's Theater) to see the ballet with Anna and Elisabetta. After the ballet, we visited Piassa Roma to see Palazzo Ducale late at night, which is a breathtaking and beautiful sight. We finally arrived home very late and I was shocked to realize these extremely late nights before working the following day is common in Italy.

Only a few days in, I realized that the smorgasbord of food and drinks set out on the table for breakfast was going to be there each morning, along with my little percolator so I could make three cups of espresso to get me moving each morning. Toast, jams, cakes, cookies, meats, cheeses, yogurt, fruits, and more were always set out for breakfast in a beautiful presentation each morning. I was so used to taking coffee to go that I saved a to-go cup from one of our meetings with VLC so I could enjoy my espresso(s) on my walk to my school each morning. I learned that go-cups were not common in Italy … one more example of conserving resources and the environment.

Mealtime was one thing I thought I was prepared for, as I grew up in the south with Sunday dinners, soul food, and family reunions, holidays, and get-togethers that require the rental of a church fellowship hall. Boy, was I wrong. They continued to have large breakfast spreads each morning with the cakes, cookies, espresso, juice, yogurt, breads, espresso, pastries, fruits, and more espresso. My family entertained 3-course lunches in the middle of the day and again in the evening. My first trip to my host paternal grandmother Nonna Maria's house ended in me feeling as if I had eaten the best four meals of my life sitting right there at her dining room table for two hours and wishing it was appropriate to pack up Tupperware containers for me to enjoy her 6-course dinner for the days to come.

Even eating out at a restaurant was a bit of a shock. Our first pizza night we had with our collegiate group, we each chose what type of pizza we wanted and ordered from the menu. When the pizzas arrived at our table, our eyes were as big as pepperonis and we belly-laughed at the size of our pizza portions. They were HUGE! (*This did not deter us from eating these fine Italian foods, however, and we could clear the plate within two weeks of our arrival.*) The thing I loved the most about dining in Italy was the social dynamics surrounding it. Everyone—both at home or at restaurants—talked, laughed, shared food, passed dishes around, and genuinely enjoyed each other's company sometimes for hours on end.

At the end of my first week in the schools, my host sister, Ceci, and her friend, Agnese, accompanied six of us from UGA to Bologna by train for an afternoon of sightseeing, gelato, and of course, shopping. We enjoyed being able to stroll down the streets of Bologna, take a look at the leaning towers, and catch up with our fellow study abroad friends with the sweet, cool, and super-fun new Italian friends! We had to get back to Modena early so some of the students could go home and pack for Venice, but my family had other plans. My family, along with Claire, went to see my host brother, Francesco, play music at a sort of a concert/music gig event. This was the first time my host family went somewhere all together and it made me feel even more welcomed into their lives. Claire and I enjoyed hearing the music and even hearing some familiar tunes in English, while also experiencing one of the most shocking revelations of the trip – not all restrooms in Italy have toilets. It was the first of many locations that had a "public restroom" that consisted of a porcelain square with two imprints of feet that show you where to stand above a hole in the ground. That first "hole potty" sighting and experience will forever remain with me.

The following week, I learned that my cinque anni class had P. E. one day per week at a roller skating rink that was about a 15-minute walk through a park from our school. I was excited to find out about this weekly "field trip" and had fun watching the instructors play games with the students and having the kids skate through obstacle courses. When we arrived back at the school, one of the teachers told me it was my time to teach and let me lead the class in some Basic English calendar time, music activities, and dances! These activities were tough at first, because none of the teachers or students spoke English, but I believe they helped me become a better teacher because I had to learn how to model instruction for students with detail and purpose. It was then that the English-speaking teacher alerted me that we would be going on a field trip the following week to visit an elementary school—the school that many of the students of the cinque anni class would be attending the following year.

A few friends and I decided we wanted to go to Parma to discover real Parmesan cheese, so we set off to the train station and bought a ticket to Parma. We took our first unaccompanied train ride (only American students—no professors, Italian host families, or program coordinator with us) and successfully found Parma, although many places were closed in the afternoon. We found a restaurant that sold parmesan cheese and chianti and picked a table outside on the patio to sit and indulge in a typical Italian lunch consisting of cheese, balsamic, and wine.

When my cinque anni class went on the field trip to the elementary school, I was not sure what to expect. We walked through the park to the school and the first year students (6–7 year olds) had written letters to the cinque anni class and drawn pictures for them. Their classes had some decorations, but far less from those in the lower school. The students were seated at desks, rather than tables, and it seemed that they did a great deal of paper/pencil work, but it was possible just the time of the day we visited. There were projects displayed in the halls from all grades and art and English projects were on display, as well. The elementary school was much more like the school I was used to seeing in the United States than my host preschool.

My family gave me the best experience possible in Modena and around northern Italy. Together, we went to the International Market in Modena's city center, which had tents set up along the cobblestone streets with foods, drinks, and crafts from Italy, Greece, Germany, Poland, Slovenia, Croatia, Frances, Switzerland, and beyond. Down the street, Piazza Giacomo Matteotti was transformed into an international outdoor food court. There were booths offering food and drink from a host of countries, such as Ireland, the United States of America, Poland, Germany, Spain, and Austria. I chose to visit the German tent with a friend of my host family and it did not disappoint. Later that night, another UGA student's host sister invited us to join her and some of her friends for drinks and dancing, so we went to one of the outdoor beer gardens in the greenway surrounding the city center.

Some of the most amazing experiences we were able to experience as students in Italy were the weekend trips we took as a group. Our classmates took trips to Venice and Florence together as well as having "free weekends" to travel on our own or with our host families.

In Venice we quickly settled into our hostel and five of us meandered the streets gazing across the canals, watching the gondoliers, and eventually landing at a restaurant for pizza and with a canal view. We later met our group at Piazza San Marco to tour the Doge's Palace, Palazzo Ducale. At sunset we took a gondola tour. The following morning the group took a boat tour to the island of Murano to watch a glass blower boast and demonstrate his craft.

Our weekend in Florence was like a dream. We arrived Friday evening and explored the city a bit before waking up Saturday morning for our day of pasta making and wine tasting. We drove out to a Tuscan estate with the owner, Maila, to learn how to make homemade pasta (fettuccini noodles and spinach/cheese ravioli) and enjoy lunch together while looking out across the Tuscan hills. Maila was incredibly sweet and patient with us while we learned to make the pasta and scribbled down the ingredients while we made them. It was one of the most delicious meals I had on the trip and what made it more interesting was the fact that we helped make it! The views of the city from Michelangelo's Lookout were unrivaled and I knew that when I was back with my parents in a few weeks, we would definitely visit this sight again. Touring the Uffizi and the Galleria dell'Accademia made the art that we had only previously seen in books and studied in high school and university classes come to life.

On my final weekend with the Ferrari's, my entire host family—Fabrizio, Anna, Cecilia, Francesco, and myself, along with my classmate Lindsey, took a trip to Ravenna, a town in eastern Italy, just minutes from the Adriatic Sea. Ravenna is the former capital of the Western Roman Empire until the empire collapsed in 476. We were all able to walk around, shop, and be tourists together. My family was able to tour churches, such as the Basilica di San Vitale, see the Mausoleo di Galla Placidia, visit the tomb of Dante (built in 1790), walk through Piazza del Popolo, and visit the Arian Baptistry to admire the mosaic ceiling. The day was perfect—especially spending the time with my entire Ferreri family, and was capped off by a visit to the famous Risorante Ca de Ven, where we enjoyed piadinas and wine before heading back to Modena.

At the end of the study abroad trip many tears were shed as the bus pulled out of the parking lot on the way to the Bologna airport. I cried, even though I was only leaving for a week-long trip to London. Afterwards, I would meet up with my own parents in Milan and we would all return to Modena. I showed my parents around Modena, the city center, took them to see my school and was surprised when I realized it was a weekday and my students were there! Walking up to the school, one of the children began yelling and shouting my name which was followed by a chorus of Shelly! Shelly! Shelly! from the cinque anni class who were playing in the courtyard at the time. My host teachers invited us inside and met my parents, then corralled the students to introduce themselves to my parents one at a time using English! Some even announced some of their favorite things using English they had been practicing.

We walked from the school to the Ferrari's house to meet some of the Ferrari family. That evening, both the Gleaton family and the Ferrari family gathered together at La Secchia Rapita for dinner, gifts, and to get to know one another over the most delicious steak on the planet. Over dinner my fathers bonded while discussing cars and my host father gave us recommendations for Maranello and the Ferrari test drive experience and Ferrari museum where we would go the following day.

After our time in Maranello and at the Enzo Ferrari museum in Modena, my host father picked us up to visit a balsamic museum, which was more like visiting a winery. My host father arranged with his friend to take us on a tour of his acetaia, which is just outside Modena. He showed us the balsamic "factory", walked us through the process of making balsamic vinegar, took us to the tasting room, and showed us around the property where the villa sits. The acetaia and property boasts stunning views, delicious balsamic, and the tour was lovely and informative. We were sure to leave with a few bottles to bring back to the United States.

On my final night in Modena, before my family left to visit southern Italy, we went to dinner at Nonna Maria's with the Ferrari family and Concetta, one of Ceci's friends. This was the first time my parents met Nonna Maria, who does not speak English. My father, who is hard-of-hearing and does not speak Italian, is very friendly and talked and talked through the entire visit. Nonna Maria continued telling stories in Italian through the meal. Nonna Maria prepared many traditional Italian dishes, including meats, cheeses, lasagna, rosetta, tortellini, and more, topped off with three dessert courses. After the first course of meats and cheeses, my dad mentioned how delicious the food was and how much he enjoyed it, to which Cecilia responded, "this is what you may call happy hour." Almost immediately, Nonna Maria brought out the lasagna and filled our plates.

While he and Nonna Maria do not speak the same language, the language of food prevailed and she realized he really liked her lasagna, so she served him another helping. Daddy said, "Oh, thank you, but I'm really full," which caused most of the table to erupt in laughter and me saying sono pieno (I am full) through laughter with Ceci. Little did he know, but he had 2–3 more dinner courses and 3 desserts before Nonna Maria had served everything on the nightly menu. The real showstopper was the delicious rosette Nonna Maria prepared. This easily became my most favorite dish I had in all my time in Italy (which Nonna Maria taught me how to make when I returned the following summer!) and consists of pasta, cheese, and ham. After thoroughly stuffing ourselves far more than we ever had at an American Thanksgiving meal, we hugged Nonna Maria and the rest of the Ferrari family and had to say our final goodbyes. Through tears, I was saying goodbye to my loving grandmother, Nonna Maria, my silly and hardworking brother, Francesco, my honest and dear parents, Fabrizio and Anna, and my sweet and social little sister, Ceci. My dad walked over to give Nonna Maria a hug and said, "You have a lovely home and we really enjoyed our dinner tonight. Thank you for everything, it was delicious." Almost immediately, we all turned to see Nonna Maria's reaction, which was a confused look with a loud "huh?" The family all doubled over in laughter which made leaving not as hard. I left them announcing ci vediamo l'anna prossimo, and I truly meant that I would see them next summer!

Note

1. Shelly Gleaton Blair, Kindergarten Teacher, Walton County (Georgia) School System.

PART THREE

Inspiration

The majority of American students who elect to participate in the UGA/Modena Schools study aboard program are pre-service teachers, each at different junctures in their professional training and development. Their plans are to graduate with an early childhood or middle grades education degree and teach in American elementary or middle schools. Throughout their university schooling they remain focused on this end result and objective.

Over the years there have been many study abroad participants whose professional visions and aspirations broaden during the experience. Certainly, all return with new ideas for teaching and inspired to incorporate more creativity and child-centered learning into their pedagogy ... elements emphasized by the Reggio approach. But there are those each year that hear the beat of a different drummer. Their aspirations dare to extend beyond anticipated teaching roles, and they see the possibility of doors opening in a variety of directions. They are inspired by the possibilities of new directions and reenergized for the career that looms before them. New decisions for moving forward are debated until they feel right and appropriate. Clyne and Rizvi (1998) offer evidence that 60% of students involved in a survey on the outcomes of student exchanges altered their plans for the future after participating in a study abroad program, and McMillan and Opem (2005) report that 90% of participants in a survey by the Institute for the

International Education of Students indicated that their international experience had influenced all subsequent educational experiences.

These students return home with a new and more direct focus for their teacher training. They set into motion any and all necessary requirements for their newly determined professional direction, having been inspired by the experience. These newly discovered revelations move beyond the American students, creating a ripple effect that engulfs host families and inspires them with their own new goals and aspirations. All move forward with excitement and commitment for something they didn't see coming.

Taylor, Megan, the Ferrari family, Chelsea, and Jordan found inspiration in unexpected places and through unexpected experiences. Two found the inspiration to venture far from home in search of career goals. The study abroad experience assured them of their competency to get by on their own. One changed her career plans completely, while one took note of what would be fundamental in her own classroom due to her own not so comfortable experiences in her Italian classroom. Taylor was so taken by the bonds created with her host family that she returned the following year to work as my student assistant in the program. The Ferrari family was inspired to improve their English language skills. The pizza, the wine, and the Italian architecture lured the girls there, and the interest of hosting American students convinced the Ferraris to sign up. None anticipated the elements of inspiration that were on the horizon.

References

Clyne, R., & Rizvi, F. A. (1998). Outcomes of student exchange. In D. Davis, & A. Olsen (Eds.), *Outcomes of international education* (pp. 35–49). Sydney: IDP Education Australia.

McMillan, A. R., & Opem, G. (2005). Study abroad: A lifetime of benefits. *Abroad View.* Retrieved from http://www.iesabroad.org/IES/About_IES/IES_News/Article/newsArtile0012.html

CHAPTER NINE

Turning Lemons into Lemonade

TAYLOR YORK[1]

I am reminded of Modena, Italy every single day. It has little to do with the balsamic vinegar or breathtaking sights, and everything to do with the people I met there. For one month, I joined a big, crazy, loving, Italian family. I ate the best food I have ever had, met some of the friendliest people in the world, and made meaningful connections with people without sharing a language. I grew as a student, as an educator, and as an individual in ways that I never expected from a study abroad opportunity.

I could fill countless pages with descriptions of my incredible host family, the delicious food and wine I tasted, and the picturesque scenery I encountered daily. While those are the experiences that made me fall in love with Modena and all of Italy, they are not the experiences that left the biggest impact. It was both the positive and the negative interactions I had with Italians that did not speak any English that challenged me to reflect on my own values and perceptions of people in general. The biggest lesson I learned over the course of that month, and the one that continues to guide me after returning to life in the states, is the importance of attitude.

During the time I lived in Modena, I was more sleep-deprived and drained of energy than I have ever been in my life. The program delivered a calendar full of school tours, day trips, and weekend excursions throughout Italy that left me exhausted and thankful. It was easy to fall into complaining about a blister or the limited sleep gotten the night before. But these were insignificant consequences of the incredible, life-changing experience before me. I approached each day and each new adventure with a positive attitude and uncharacteristic flexibility. I took advantage of the bus rides between towns to catch up on sleep so that I might be able to stay up a few minutes longer to watch a movie with my host dad or to tuck in my siblings. When staying awake seemed impossible, I excused myself to the bathroom where I would do jumping jacks to make myself wake up. I was not about to let lack of sleep or homesickness interfere with my incredible adventure.

My host siblings and I spent many nights teaching each other the names of animals, numbers, and everyday objects in our native languages. My very first night I was left with them and my grandpa, none of whom spoke English. I can still hear my sister laughing at her grandpa's effort to ask me if I would like an egg with dinner by doing the chicken dance and repeatedly acting out cracking an egg. My host dad's mother was so excited to meet me and cook lunch for me that she tried to learn a little English via Google Translate in order to personally welcome me into her home. When we arrived at her house the next day for lunch, she opened the front door with a giant smile and waved, "bye bye!". Not realizing the error in her translation of "ciao," she ran up to hug me, leaving me confused as to whether or not I was allowed in her home. When my dad corrected her she burst out laughing and began speaking in rapid Italian while I smiled and nodded at the one or two words I understood. The majority of the people I encountered were so welcoming and willing to dance around words in order to communicate with me.

My love for my host family was not unique. Year after year the majority of participants in this program are introduced to the perfect Italian family they never knew they had. I was worried that I would feel isolated and uncomfortable living with a host family for a month, and instead I was a crying mess when I left them. I was placed with a family that was perfect for me, where I could thrive during this Italian adventure and feel right at home.

One of my biggest worries going into this trip was the inherent language barrier. Ignoring the strong advice of the program director, I never so much as cracked the spine of the Italian workbook we had been given until our layover at JFK. Consequently, it was safe to say I was not confident in my ability to communicate with Italians. I knew that my host family spoke some English, but I was somewhat worried about their fluency based on the emails we exchanged. We were told in pre departure sessions that the language barrier was a vital part of the study abroad experience. We would learn ways to communicate without oral language, and we would experience firsthand the strangeness and isolation of being a non-native speaker. As future educators, these experiences would give us a deeper perspective of non-English speaking students and better prepare us for working with them in our American classrooms.

My school placement during the program was in a fourth grade classroom in a school near my host family's apartment. I had prepared activities and had communicated with them about my excitement to meet them and learn about Italian schools. I was welcomed on my first day with a colorful sign on the chalkboard reading, "Welcome, Taylor!" followed by English introductions from each of the students and the teacher. I would be assisting the students with English and helping them prepare for their play *The Wizard of Oz*. The first day at recess the children taught me some Italian games and asked me questions about America. Later, with translation help from the math teacher, I told them about myself and my life in the US.

The rest of my school experience was not quite as positive as that first day. Instead of facing that challenge of a language barrier, my teachers ignored me. As a result of not being engaged and not understanding the language in the classroom, I became bored and disinterested. I felt my presence did not matter. I connected to discussions from my university courses about pushing children aside and depriving them of voice from my experience sitting in the corner of the classroom. Day after day I was left to question my purpose in the classroom. At recess I interacted with my students, practiced my limited Italian, and began to understand how universally similar children are. When the students did not understand what I said or vice versa, we would work our way around words using gestures and other resources eventually understanding one another. I interacted with a blind student and learned the Italian method for long division from another student using a mixture of basic English and Italian.

Part of me kept hoping that the experience with my teachers would improve at school, and I would be able to contribute in the ways that I had anticipated. Realizing that this was unlikely to be the case, I began to see the value and difficulty and negativity of the situation. It required a change in my attitude and taking on a new direction. This was an opportunity to sit back and reflect on how I felt when I was ignored by teachers. Each day I took my personal journal to school and I would use my time to catch up on descriptions of weekend trips and reflect on how I was feeling. This was my personal challenge to turn lemons into lemonade. When my school placement did not turn out to be ideal, I did learn from it. The experience helped shape who I am as both a teacher and an individual.

Only months later, in my school placement back in the US, I drew upon my Italian classroom experience while helping a non-English speaking student in my class with math. I noticed a change in his attitude right away. He was willing to try to finish his work and to communicate with me. Normally sad and serious he even began joking with me. Sitting beside him during our first math session, I thought about my Italian teachers and was determined to make every effort with him. I used my limited Spanish and big smiles to let him know that I cared and that he was welcomed in my classroom. I know that my own personal experience gave me the drive to make that student feel welcomed, noticed and capable of learning.

This opportunity was enough to remind me to be purposeful in my teaching of students and to always except the challenge of communication rather than ignore it. It reminds me to value the wisdom and experience that my students bring to the classroom and to help them realize that language is only one method of communicating with others. I am reminded of how often they are misunderstood, have hurt feelings, and fail to speak up for themselves. I have personally experienced the result of "silencing" children with language barriers and challenges. My month in the corner of the Italian classroom resulted in a personal promise to my future students to see them, recognize them, and work with them to overcome any and all obstacles.

Note

1. Taylor York, 4th Grade Teacher, Fulton County (Georgia) School System.

CHAPTER TEN

Independence—Who Knew?

MEGAN GREENE[1]

Throughout my high school and college coursework I developed an immense interest in international education and educational policy. I studied various education philosophies and models, and while I have seen some in action in the American schools, I yearned to explore such models globally. The college of education's study abroad program in Modena, Italy gave me this opportunity. There I would live with an Italian host family, work in local schools, and see firsthand the famed Reggio approach to early learning. The program greatly exceeded my expectations.

Acceptance into the study abroad program required a great deal of personal information which was used to match me with a host family. I answered questions about my hobbies, family, aspirations, diet, and more. Being gluten intolerant, this was a major concern for me; after all, pasta and pizza are staples of the Italian diet! Intentionally, I was matched with a family who followed a gluten-free diet. Additionally, the family mirrored my own. When I received my family assignment, I was surprised to learn that my host father was an engineer like my father, the host mother was involved in schools like my mother, and the kids were in high school and college, just like my brother and me. We also shared interests like hiking and music! It was a perfect match.

From day one I immersed myself into the community and culture. I truly lived like a local—eating traditional dishes with my host family, commuting via bus or bike, and more. Living with a host family truly amplified this experience and set this program apart from other study abroad programs I had researched. Aside from introducing me to their customs, they conversed with me about my academic interests. My host siblings were in high school and college so I heard about their educational past and their opinions on the Italian school system. My host mother was a neuropsychiatrist and worked with students with special needs, and so we compared the treatment of special needs students in Italy with those in America. My host father was an engineer and often travels to other European countries, so he shared his international work experience with me. I'm incredibly thankful to have been placed with my host family, as they enriched my experience immensely.

When I left Italy I was unaware that my bond with my host family would continue. Just a month later, my host siblings came to visit me in the states, and I had the opportunity to show them around Athens! Afterwards, we stayed in touch, talking nearly every day and Skyping from time to time, and nearly a year later, my host sister came to stay with me. We visited my parents, grandparents, Atlanta, and Athens. I enjoyed being the host instead of the visitor! I do not know when I will be able to return to Italy, but I know that I am always welcome and that I truly have an Italian family.

Though I only spent four hours a day for three and a half weeks working in an Italian school, my teaching experience was invaluable. The school staff was very gracious, and my English mentor teacher allowed me to lead the class nearly every day. One day I taught for four hours straight! I had not at that point had such an opportunity during my American school placements. Additionally, I could tell that my lessons were effective. I spent some free time drawing on the board and writing the names of various animals in English. While this was not designated as an academic lesson, I later noticed that one of the students took out her English notebook and copied down some of the terms. I also had a blast teaching my students about body parts. I drew a picture of a person on the chalkboard and the students helped me label and pronounce each part in Italian and English. They were eager to copy the diagram in their English notebooks. Afterwards we went outside and did the hokey pokey! They loved singing the song and dancing so much that they never realized they were using their newly learned English vocabulary. I also taught the English alphabet, American food, clothing, and animals. I am so grateful for my opportunities to teach as they inspired me to pursue my ESOL (English as a second language) endorsement when I return to UGA.

On occasion I stayed for school lunch. Several students spent the entire lunch trying to communicate with me via limited English, hand gestures, and facial expressions. These experiences made me realize the importance of the conversational component of second-language learning. The students learned a lot just by communicating with me in an informal setting, while I absorbed the dynamics of an Italian school lunch. The school lunches are delicious! Lasagna was served family style. Students serve each other and use their manners graciously. During lunch students talk and laugh and play—not forced to eat silently. I was intrigued by lunchtime and the entire structure and dynamics of a typical Italian school day. Many classes incorporate themes based on student interests, and standards and objectives are integrated naturally. Art and music are heavily integrated into the curriculum, and there are classes in religion and baking. Additionally, parents and community members are heavily involved in the school benefiting students and teachers.

Of special interest to me was the opportunity to visit preschools that incorporate the Reggio approach to early learning. Having previously studied the approach in my UGA classes, I was excited to see it in action. This was an authentic opportunity to connect theory and practice. My first impression of the schools was their beauty. There were no cinderblock walls covered with standards and objectives. Instead, schools were colorful, windows were everywhere, student work and photographs were displayed, and resources were abundant. Schools felt safe, happy, and welcoming. Most of the classrooms had more than one teacher. This collaboration seemed to help both the teachers and the students. Additionally, the teachers' roles were starkly different from those of American teachers. Instead of transmitting content as quickly as possible, teachers served as guides for student-centered learning. They focused on student interests and actively interacted with the children in the classroom.

Italian families were involved in Reggio pre-schools and elementary schools. Parents drop their children off and pick them up every day, sometimes even visiting for lunch or stopping in for a lesson. The teachers view parents as a resource to help increase student achievement and success. Parents and teachers are friends. While continuing my studies at UGA I have had opportunities to share this valuable knowledge and experience with my peers.

After completion of the four-week study abroad program, I elected to stay and work as a camp counselor in an English summer camp program. I thought this experience would be simply a continuation of my work in the Italian schools, but it was a different and enriching experience. Instead of shadowing talented teachers, I was in charge! I worked with first and second grade students. The language barrier was a challenge. Some days I had an Italian teenage assistant, but I was mostly on my own. My young students had yet to learn much English other than simple words like colors, numbers, foods, and basic introduction words. When a student was feeling sick or upset, we had to communicate without language. Because of this, discipline was extremely hard. I learned words like stop, listen, relax, and sit down, but I had trouble understanding the reasoning behind a student's behavior. These challenges did not limit my enjoyment of the summer camp. I could tell that the students valued English and were eager to learn. They loved listening to my English music and reading books with me. We ended each day by sharing our new word of the day. After ten days, I know that my students learned at least ten new words, but I believe that most of them learned more!

While I learned a lot about education during this experience, I also learned a great deal about myself. For the first time in my life, I was in the minority. I was very apprehensive about ordering food, shopping, using public transportation, etc. Even when I knew the correct words, my American accent gave me away as an outsider. However, during an excursion to Venice, I went into a store and made my purchase using only Italian. The shopkeeper spoke English to the customer before and after me, but seemed to think I was a local! I was very proud. Experiences such as this helped me develop empathy and understanding for how minorities in the US and in my classroom must feel on a daily basis.

I became more independent. I hardly knew any of the other study abroad participants before we departed. This was one of the first times in my life that I was going somewhere without a friend or family member. I was very nervous, but I easily adjusted to my host family and peers. I made lifelong friends, and I developed a lasting bond with my host family. I also enjoyed being independent. I went shopping on my own in Modena one afternoon and learned to navigate the city. When I returned to the US, I no longer felt the need to bring a friend with me to a social event or even on a trip. I recently flew to New York City and visited many tourist sites completely alone. Next year, I plan to move to a new city to begin my teaching career, and it is likely that I will not know anyone there. Once frightful of this, I now feel confident. And I know that I will easily adjust, and honestly, I enjoy the independence, something I never saw coming.

I chose the UGA/ Modena School Study abroad program because it supported my future goals, but it opened my eyes to new ones. After successfully teaching Italian students I feel confident that I could be an ESOL teacher for students of any linguistic background. Where I once had reservations I have gained a first-hand perspective of the struggles of a second language learner. I can now more accurately understand how ESOL students feel in schools. And I believe I can be more sensitive to their academic and social needs. Working in the Italian school has pushed me to complete my ESOL endorsement. In American schools I have worked with students from various linguistic background: lobo, Spanish, and Romanian. I was proud of my ability to help beginning English speakers be successful in the classroom. The techniques and skills I learned in Italy were invaluable as I differentiated lessons for those non-native speaking students.

My experiences in Italy increased my desire and confidence to teach internationally. I am considering participating in the Fulbright teaching exchange program after teaching in the US for several years. My interest in educational policy has also been increased. I learned about schools in other countries and spoke with my host family about laws and policies. I am impressed by the success of Italian and Reggio Schools, and I think that many of their principles can be effective in US schools. I am interested to learn more about schools in other countries, as well. I believe that American schools can learn from other countries. I hope to travel again in the future and use what I learned to impact public schools in America. I also plan to complete a doctoral degree in education, and I am considering a degree in international education policy.

The study abroad experience changed me as a person: academically, socially, and personally. I am proud of the impact that I made on Italian students, but I am even more thankful for the impact they and my Italian host family made on me. For a first-time traveler, I could not have chosen a better study abroad program, country, or group of people. My eyes have been opened to all that awaits.

Note

1. Megan Greene, 3rd Grade Teacher, District of Columbia Public Schools.

CHAPTER ELEVEN

Learning from Our Children

FERRARI FAMILY (ANNA, CECILIA, FABRIZIO, FRANCESCO)[1]

Our first hosting experience was in 2012 following the advice of another family that had hosted the previous year. Our first student was the kind Jennifer, a very polite, delicate, and sensitive girl. She immediately became part of our family, as if she had always lived with us. As soon as she arrived we were no longer parents of two children, but three. We never had difficulties understanding her needs (they were very few). We did not expect that hosting and interacting with other girls in the group would be so simple.

2012 was a very peculiar year. It was the year of the terrible earthquake in Modena and its province and having Jenny with us certainly helped us in dealing with this event better. We were faced with a situation of being always together, along with other American girls, our children's friends, grandparents, other parents, and so on. If we had not been hosting American girls, I think the earthquake would have been much harder to deal with. We were able to redirect our tensions by focusing on them and not so much on our fearful situation. They provided inspiration for moving forward and enjoying each day to the fullest. It was also very useful and inspiring to practice the English language, especially for children. So, when Jenny left us to return home, we were all so very sad.

Inspired by our relationship with Jenny and renewed interests in English, several months later Cecilia went to Malta to participate in an English course and

Francesco to Ghana with an international voluntary association. Jenny had left us with curiosity, wonderings, and new goals.

The following year Shelly came, the fantastic and enthusiastic Shelly. She was very different from Jenny, but immediately in tune with our habits and our lives. She was very agile, organized, independent but very close to us, super nice and loving. She was a lover of good food who went several times to attend kitchen lessons with her grandmother Maria. She learned quickly and became a specialist in cooking "rosette" which she continues to prepare in Georgia. Shelly entered our family and our hearts. She is like a daughter to us. She came to Italy for three consecutive years, and for us it was always a great joy to welcome her. She said she felt like she was one of our daughters and that she could have stayed with us forever. In 2016 she got married and invited us all, but only Cecilia could attend. We later went to the seaside together and spent a few days in New York. As a family and as a parent we can confirm that this hosting experience has enriched us greatly and has inspired new opportunities for growth and knowledge.

Note

1. Ferrari Family (Anna, Cecilia, Fabrizio, Francesco), Italy Host Family.

CHAPTER TWELVE

The Power of Communication

CHELSEA LYNN WALKER[1]

Nearly four years, two degrees, and a number of educational experiences later, I continue to embrace the memories and feel the impact of my experiences in Modena, Italy. What drew me to this particular study abroad experience was the opportunity to live with a host family and work in Italian schools. Soon after deciding to participate in the program, I changed my major to communication sciences and disorders with the intentions of going to graduate school for speech-language pathology. My parents, who have always been supportive of my decisions, asked a great question, "How does this trip to Italy working in schools have anything to do with Speech-Language pathology?" Great question, parents. And challenge accepted. It was my mission to make this experience meaningful and applicable to my future. Two months later I landed in Italy, hopped on the bus with all the other study abroad students, and arrived in Modena, my home for the next month. The first few days were a whirlwind. I thought I was prepared for what was to come. I had asked multiple questions at our pre-departure sessions, looked up translations for basic vocabulary, communicated with my host family and asked them relevant questions, and I packed everything on my list. Truth is, culture shock is a real thing, no matter how prepared you are.

My host family immersed me in the culture from the very first minute. As soon as I arrived, it was time for dinner with their friends to welcome me to Italy. I sat around the table with a group of Italian speaking adults. The only one who spoke fluent English was my host mother. She did her best to translate, but there's only so much one can do. I learned two very important things that first day: (1) this experience was going to be way more than I bargained for and (2) I should have studied more Italian before the trip.

A couple of days later I found myself walking into an elementary school, meeting second grade teachers and twenty-something second graders who would be my class for the next few weeks. I sat in the back of the classroom observing with an English/Italian dictionary in hand, trying to figure out what they were saying. Math was my favorite lesson to observe. Turns out, numbers look the same in Italian as they do in English. When the students worked independently, I walked around the room and helped them as much as I could given the language barrier. I stopped at one student's desk. I began speaking slowly, gesturing, pointing, doing anything I could to communicate. She looked at me quizzically and then informed me that she understood me—she spoke English. I've never been so excited to hear those words.

The group also had incredible opportunities to visit other schools outside our assigned placement in Modena in order to witness firsthand the famed Reggio approach to early learning. We toured a local preschool that was AMAZING. I cannot explain how creative, crafty, intense, welcoming, fun, and every other adjective one would want a preschool to be described as the school was. Every single artifact on the walls had a purpose and was created by a little one. What did I love most about the school? The fact that children were surrounded by opportunities to use and display their creativity.

In less than a week I was practically a local. Between touring city landmarks, meeting city officials, eating at local restaurants, and being photographed for an Italian newspaper, I felt at home in no time. Wow! I quickly recognized how different Italian culture was from American, but I began to realize the similarities, as well. I felt as much at home as I could, being halfway across the world from my real home.

A few days later I met with the other study abroad girls for our weekly meeting. These meetings were a favorite part of the week. They were a time when I could speak fast in English, not have to repeat myself, and share my struggles with people who were in the same boat. We worked together to prepare lessons to teach our classes centered on fairytales. Most of the Italian children have heard the fairytales in their own language, so we thought this familiarity would help them to better understand when presented in English. My lesson was near perfect, so I thought. After reading the first page of my selected fairytale, I looked up to see 20+ faces in total confusion. I learned a valuable lesson about teaching that day—flexibility and meeting children where they are. I regrouped, consulted my

Italian-English dictionary, and prepared a list of key vocabulary from the fairytale in English and Italian. Reading the fairytale in English very slowly and stopping after each page to discuss the key vocabulary in both languages, transformed the children from confusion to engagement. The lesson was not at all what I had originally planned and envisioned, but it proved successful and meaningful and taught me the importance of flexibility in teaching.

Outside of my experiences with my class and with the other members of the study abroad group, I had special opportunities with my host family. A day in the hillside celebrating my host brother's birthday, delicious meals around the kitchen table, long talks with my host mom about all the things that one discusses with a mom, running errands, arguments, sitting with my host mom in the emergency room while she was being treated for a poisonous snake bite, and movie nights are only a few of the unbelievable experiences we had together. We shared the experiences that real families share. I can say that living with a host family was not something I was excited about when I enrolled in the program. Living with strangers who do not speak your language seemed an odd situation to me. However, when I finally let go of my preconceived notions and dove in headfirst, I came out with a unique perspective and remarkable second family. Life is always an adventure with them. We still keep in touch from time to time, and I am often reminded of how blessed I was for an opportunity to be a part of their lives, experience their lives, and make lifelong friends.

My four weeks in Modena flew by. When it was time to leave I was sad that my incredible adventure had come to an end. I was leaving a beautiful city, amazing memories, a beautiful culture, outstanding study abroad friends, and most of all, and an unbelievably loving and wonderful family. When I got back to Georgia, my parents greeted me with the same question, "How did this trip to Italy working in schools have anything to do with Speech-Language Pathology?" My immediate response—How did it not? I finally realized the power of communication. Words are powerful. Language is powerful. The ability to communicate is powerful. My time in Italy provided me an invaluable opportunity to walk a mile in my clients' shoes and realize the frustration and confusion that comes with the inability to communicate. Modena was my first of many invaluable experiences to walk in others' shoes. The perspectives I gained there have been invaluable in my career.

Note

1. Chelsea Lynn Walker, Pediatric Speech-Language Pathologist, Muscogee County (Georgia) School District.

CHAPTER THIRTEEN

When in Rome

JORDAN MOORE[1]

Traveling many miles to study abroad in Italy, I exchanged the comfort of my home for the unknown of living with a host family in a new culture. I left the busyness of my suburban town to live in a beautiful house settled amongst fields and mountains. I replaced drives on busy streets with walks to school with my host family. As I embraced these new experiences, I learned how to slow down and appreciate what was around me.

After arriving in Italy, I was immediately fascinated by the Italian culture and my Italian family's way of life. I found myself snapping pictures as an attempt to capture the beauty that I found, but a picture does not let you smell the scent in the air of fresh flowers or let you hear the songs of the birds and the crickets. We collect pictures as a way to document an experience, a way to archive it and share it with others, but I learned in my month that a picture does not capture the truest aspects of the experience. When I show people pictures of the Alps, they see the two-dimensional beauty. They can see the blue sky and the contrast between the green grass and white rocks, but they are unable to feel the breeze, smell the aromas or see the birds dancing in the air. My experience studying abroad in Italy for a month was an experience that goes beyond a camera lens. During the month I experienced many places. I climbed to the top of city towers and saw castles for the first time. I walked on streets that dated back hundreds of years and saw mountains and seasides that looked like paintings. But beyond all the beautiful places, the best part of the experience was the relationships I built with my host family and class.

There is something beautiful about strangers opening their home to you. Out of place, in a country where I did not speak the language, I found myself dependent on a family that I had just met. The views of the mountains and streets of Venice fail to even remotely compare with the moments I spent with my family. On just my sixth night in Modena, after coming back from eating pizza with the group, my host father told me it was strange not having me with them at dinner. In that moment, a sense of joy and belonging swelled up within me. To know that this family had welcomed me in such an unconditional way in just a matter of days touched my heart so deeply. Throughout the month, we spent more time together sharing bits of our culture with each other. On the weekends, I had the opportunity to be a tourist, taking selfies on gondola rides and visiting museums, but at the end of each weekend, I looked forward to coming back to my Italian home.

Some of my favorite memories with my host family include sharing long meals where we sat around and enjoyed each other's company or staying up late into the night talking about anything and everything. Even though we lived in different places and spoke different languages, we often ended these conversations realizing that we were more similar than different. We were able to share bits of our culture with each other. On one of my favorite nights, we gathered as an extended family to grill outside. They shared with me different types of foods, and I introduced them to s'mores. My host mom later shared that this experience made her happy because she never thought she would see her father eat a marshmallow. I found that since we were living together, we were all very open to learning about and experiencing each other's culture.

While I feel like I got to know my host family well, I realized that my experience was unique and would not necessarily transfer to living with another Italian family. Consequently, I embraced the experience of living with my chosen Italian family, and appreciated the fact that all host families and Italian families are different. I found myself learning to value my host family for who they were as individuals.

Before I arrived, my host family had described themselves as "simple people that lived in a garden." This description could not have been more perfect. Coming from a hometown where people focus on filling their lives with things and a hectic lifestyle, it was refreshing to experience a new way of life. They share a home with their extended family. Everything in the home has a place and nothing is excessive. Trash is sorted and recycled, and there is little waste. Conservation guides their daily routines. They live a few minutes outside the city center and their home is situated on a gravel road that parallels a beautiful field. The family gathers in the yard on weekends to talk and play together. My Italian home was perfect. It was different from my suburban home in Georgia, but it provided me a beautiful opportunity to experience living life in a different way. They live their lives in a way that I hope to live mine, so to experience this was an incredible opportunity that gave me a sense of hope that it is possible to live simply in the world.

Most nights I found myself staring out the window of our third story flat, endlessly captivated and fascinated by the way the trees, mountains, and sky came together. I stood there in front of the screened window smelling the sweet breeze as it blew in the open window of my room each night. I took deep breaths as I tried to fill my lungs with the air, knowing that my month was passing by much too quickly.

Living in such a beautiful place forced me to pause and slow down for the first time in many years. The combination of new experiences and knowing my time was limited helped me to take it all in. I also found myself without consistent internet access for the first time in many years. The first night, it felt strange going to bed without first mindlessly scrolling through my phone. I realized that this was probably the first time in many years that this was the case. Without all the constant distractions, and with the slower pace, I learned to take time and notice the environment around me. I noticed how the leaves on the trees looked and the different types of flowers I passed on my walks to school. I noticed the way the deep blue sky contrasted with the warm orange colored buildings. I noticed the way the gravel road felt under my feet. I noticed the words on the signs I passed as I tried to make sense of them. It was easy in a new place to do this, because there were plenty of things to observe. Eventually I began to wonder what sights, sounds and sensations I was missing in my daily life in America. I promised myself that when I returned to the states I would continue this practice of noticing.

On my fourth and last weekend, we packed our bags and headed to Mount Baldo and Lake Garda. My host parents had shared early in my stay that they wanted us to go there together. It is one of their favorite places, and after only knowing me for a week they decided they would like to share it with me. The weekend was full of surreal moments. Between walking around a castle, riding a cable car, hiking, and playing in the lake, I learned how to pay better attention to the world around me. My host father is a wildlife photographer so he always takes his camera on family trips. He photographs wild animals and flowers that can be hard to find in Italy. As a family they study the different types of flowers on Mount Baldo and have been looking for some flowers for many years. Before we went, they shared with me the specific flower they had been trying to find for over ten years. I can honestly say that before this trip I had never paid much attention to flowers. My experience hiking and looking for flowers changed my perspective. I began to fully understand the adage "stop and smell the roses".

I usually walk quickly when I hike, but my host family showed me how hiking is more about the experience than the destination. In a beautiful way, I feel like this lesson was a theme of my study abroad experience—that it is about the experience, the culture and relationships that are important in life, not the destinations. As we walked along the edge of the Alps, we searched for different flowers. We noticed the deep rich colors of the blue flowers. They showed me ones that look like buttons, and I stopped and noticed one that was a tie-dye color of deep blue and purple. Finally, we found the one they were looking for. It was amazing for me to experience this joy of finding something rare and coveted that had eluded them for ten years. It was something I would have just walked past if they had not shown it to me. As we stopped so my host father could take photos, I found myself awestruck by the contrast between the enormity of the mountains and the delicateness and detail of the flowers. It was a special moment where I was captivated and amazed by creation. I remember sitting at the top of the mountain taking deep breaths, knowing that a picture could never capture the beauty.

Just as I was starting to notice the intricate details in the landscape around me, I also started to notice the nuances of the classroom in which I was placed. At first glance, the school looked so different than the schools I had seen in America, but it did not take long to see the universal nature of children, and as the month went on, I began to better understand the educational approach of the area. In the beginning, the class seemed to be disorganized and unproductive. I was frustrated at first because it did not seem to match up with the Reggio approach that we were told the schools embodied. It would have been easy to stop there and form assumptions, but by looking deeper I was able to notice other things. These first graders had the ability to stay focused for a long amount of time and manage their own problems. These are skills that have to be cultivated and encouraged from an early age. I was also able to appreciate the teachers' flexibility. Days and schedules were arranged so the teachers had the time and the ability to be flexible. This allowed opportunities for exploration and time for the class to study topics that were important to the class. Teachable moments were seldom lost or ignored.

One of my favorite moments was the school trip to a park and the teachers instructed the children to "take off their shoes and roll around in the grass." The teacher later shared with me that this activity purposefully was an activity to engage the senses. However, with all of the positives I saw, I also witnessed situations and strategies that were not as positive. At these times I realized that no education system in perfect, but I could certainly learn from different things I saw in my Italian school and take away the practices that impressed me and made sense.

As a part of working with the class, I had a few things I had prepared to do, including sharing songs, books, and games. I was able to do this, but I realized very quickly that it was important that I be engaged in more than just these simple activities. Just like paying attention to the flowers on the hike, the important part of the experience in the school was in the details. One of these important details of my experience was the way that we were able to form relationships even though we did not speak the same language. When I went on the school trip to the park, I spent the day with teachers and students that spoke very little English. Even though we could not understand each other, I did not feel out of place. I think this can be attributed to the fact that we had built a relationship and sense of understanding that went beyond our language barrier.

Thinking back to the diversity of school populations in the United States, I was reminded that it is not necessary to speak the same language in order to make someone feel welcome and to build a relationship with him. In the same way, however, someone does not automatically feel welcome. On some mornings when the class was doing worksheets and I was not engaged with the class, I was exhausted. I found it hard to stay awake if I was not engaged in some way, even if this just meant finding a student to help. I learned that we need to make sure students who do not speak English have a way they can engage with what is going on in the class. This will help them have a sense of purpose and belonging. Additionally, I learned that learning a few words can make a big difference. Just by learning a few Italian words, I was able to interact and help students in meaningful ways. In the same way, I think we can learn a few words of students' languages if it means we will be able to help them succeed.

There were two experiences during my time in the school that specifically stand out to me. The first one opened my eyes to a way I could make a difference in the classroom. There was a student in the class that was trying to help another student with special needs, but she was trying to help in a way that was manipulative and not beneficial. Watching the situation unfold, I knew that I could either watch this one student continue to get upset as the other student manipulated her hand forcefully, or I could try to intervene. I decided to try to model for this student how to help someone in a positive way. It worked out to be a positive experience, because I was able to help the student complete the worksheet without ever touching the student's hand, pencil, or paper. This was a unique experience for me because even though I could not speak his language, I was able to help the student complete a task and model for the other student ways to help a peer.

The second experience was seeing how the students grew in their understanding of communication. I was able to see a clear difference in our ability to communicate on the first day compared to the last. On the first day, the students repetitively spoke to me in Italian. Realizing I could not understand, they would just say the sentence again. They seemed to be confused about why it was diffi-cult for me to understand. By the end of my time in the classroom, they had only learned how to say some numbers, "hello," and "how are you," but we were able to find ways to communicate. When speaking to me in Italian, they spoke slowly and in isolated words, and acted out what they were trying to say. On my last day, they were able to communicate that they wanted me to play hide and seek with them and later that they wanted to borrow the notebook from my backpack to draw pictures. Even though we could not speak each other's languages, we were able to gain a deeper understanding of what it means to communicate and how to communicate with people that are different and in ways other than words.

Leaving these students after three weeks was harder than I would have ever expected. I felt so welcomed and loved in the classroom during my month. It was refreshing to focus on building relationships instead of curriculum or discipline, and I was reminded of why I chose to pursue teaching. It is easy for personal per-spectives of education to be clouded by what has to be done or the regulations that are in place on and mandated. Just like I learned on my hike in the Alps, I also saw in the classroom that it is important to pay attention to the details and the smaller moments, focus on building relationships and see what can be discovered.

Both in the classroom and throughout my experience with my host family, my experience in Italy taught me about looking for the smaller details and paying attention to the world around me. Against the backdrop of one of the most beau-tiful places I have been, I learned lessons that I believe shaped the trajectory of my life. There is something so unique and beautiful about this experience. My Italian family taught me how to notice the little things. They showed me what it looks like to live a life that values experiences over materialism. They helped me gain a desire to save and cherish every moment instead of letting them fly by. As I stood in the parking lot, about to board the bus and leave, tears streamed down my face. My host mom told me not to cry, but to instead be happy. I think she knew I was happy. I had told her that my tears were of happiness and thankfulness. Italy had changed my heart. The experience of being welcomed by a family of strangers is one for which I will forever be thankful. I gained a deep understanding of culture and its fluidity. I experienced the culture of my Italian host family. However, my experience was unique, something that no one else can recreate because my expe-rience was the result of the merging of our individual cultures, personalities, and ways of life. I was able to see life through a new lens. I believe this lens is some-thing gained with each cultural experience and that it is a way for me to better see and understand the beauty in the details in the world around me.

I left Italy with a sense that the world is bigger and in some ways smaller than I thought. Experiencing the culture and getting to know Italian people helped me recognize the realness and humanity of people across the world from me. I was struck by the realization that there are people all over the world with families and struggles; however, at the same time, this vastness of the world shrunk before my eyes as the differences that I had perceived started to disappear or seemed unimportant.

Note

1. Jordan Moore, Camp Retreat Leader, Camp Wabanna (Maryland).

Acceptance

With the outlook of spending four weeks with complete strangers, some involved with the UGA/Modena schools program prepare by cloaking themselves in a protective demeanor. They are excited about the opportunities that lie ahead, but self-preservation becomes a priority. They stop short of allowing doubts and concerns to cloud their visions and expectations, but are cautious, nevertheless, about finding themselves in vulnerable situations. They look inward and assume a stance of relying solely on themselves and not letting down their guard. Only days into the experience the armor begins to peel away. They find themselves reaching out, taking risk, seizing opportunities, and regretting that the days are flying by. This change of heart and willingness to throw caution to the wind is brought about through acceptance. Something they didn't see coming.

As the days pass they begin to embrace differences and realize that these differences are what make us who we are. Once fearful of the unknown and reluctant to step out of their comfort zones, they develop a deeper appreciation for other people, other cultures, and other ways of doing. This new attitude and approach result in the inclination to take themselves less seriously and appreciate their own talents and contributions. The feeling of acceptance is quickly reciprocated establishing productive working relationships and lasting friendships. This realization of acceptance results in a greater diversity of friends (Dwyer, 2004), an increased openness to new ideas (Nunan, 2006), and easier adaptability to new and unfamiliar situations (Orahood, Kruze, & Pearson, 2004).

The experience ends and all involved are left more confident and with renewed outlooks. Realizing the power of acceptance—of others and of themselves—results in a greater level of maturity and worldliness. This, for sure, they didn't see coming. Sara Carter, a 2017 participant, emphasized this point in the digital story she submitted after her return to the states. She explained that "my trip to Italy taught me that unexpected and unplanned events in our lives are often far better than anything we could ever plan ourselves … So thank you Italy for showing me that just being Sara is good enough and how change and the unknown are not so scary after all".

Stefania, Camilla, Bethany, and Rachel epitomize acceptance and the accomplishments that can come with it. Stefania and Camilla warmly accepted and embraced the students assigned to their classrooms and through their story reveal the rewards that come from the international match-ups when there is a willingness to reach out and accept others for who they are. Bethany accepted all that came her way and ignited in herself a wanderlust for travel and took off in many directions insisting that her own high school students literally go along for the ride and the experience.

Rachel accepted everything from day one. She never stopped smiling from the day she met with me in my office to discuss the details of the study abroad program until the present. I have the opportunity to continue to see her often since she now teaches in a school where I conduct most of my university work. Rachel will forever hold a special memory for me as a program participant. I remember so well her mom and dad bidding her goodbye at the Atlanta airport on the day we departed. She had never taken off on such an adventure before. In fact, she had never even flown before. I swallowed the lump in my throat as I saw her embrace her dad for one last hug as tears ran down their faces. I was reminded of the special feelings that dads have for their little girls. I was also reminded of my part in making the study abroad opportunity happen for Rachel and the fact that her parents were pushing aside their anxieties and thoughts of uncertainty in order for her to embark on this adventure. Only months later Rachel would lose her dad in a tragic car accident. To this day one of my most treasured memories of this study abroad program is the image of them hugging each other that day in May in the international terminal. It is one of my fondest memories from all of the years combined. I am comforted by the thought that Rachel's Italian experience with acceptance and treasuring each and every moment of her time with a host family that she continues to hold dearly gave her guidance and comfort in her time of sadness and despair.

References

Carter, S. (2017). *Italy 2017: The best unexpected trip of my life*. Retrieved from https://www.youtube.com/watch?v=zcjLqI8YBA0&feature=youtu.be

Dwyer, M. M. (2004). More is better: The impact of study abroad program duration. *Frontiers: The Interdisciplinary Journal of Study Abroad, 10*, 151–163.

Nunan, P. (2006). *An exploration of the long term effects of student exchange experiences*. Paper presented at the annual meeting of the Australian International Education Conference. Retrieved from http://aiec.idp.com/uploads/pdf/Nunan%20%28Paper%29%20Thurs@200900%20MR5.pdf

Orahood, T., Kruze, L., & Pearson, D. (2004). The impact of study abroad on business students' career goals. *Frontiers: The Interdisciplinary Journal of Study Abroad, 10*, 117–130.

CHAPTER FOURTEEN

No Regrets

STEFANIA LANCELLOTTI AND CAMILLA GIOVANARDI[1]

Maggie became a part of us, part of the class 1°A at the Giacomo Leopardi Primary School. Our children are only six or seven years old, so we had been wondering whether hosting an American student was a good decision for such small children with no fluency and no great knowledge of the foreign language. However, going beyond the linguistic aspect, we began to understand that hosting an American student is, indeed, a complete experience from our point of view. One thing is for sure. We do not know anyone who has ever regretted it!

First we should consider the linguistic aspect. The American girl assigned to our class was extremely kind, sweet, and communicative with the children. They enjoyed thinking about ways to communicate with her, like learning some basic structures to communicate or to pay her compliments since she was quite pretty. They made their researches at home, asked the English teacher for guidance, and immersed themselves into the foreign language with ease, driven by the desire to convey a message to the person that lived among us during that month. Maggie also conducted lessons on a topic I had chosen, using different types of materials and showing pictures of American schools.

Second, the cultural aspect should not be underestimated! We all know that a foreign language cannot be separated from the cultural context in which it is spoken, and if we talk about the USA, Italian kids are already strongly motivated and willing to know more! Maggie brought us photos, slides about her school, explained and taught us games in the sports hall, helped us with a little cooking workshop, and shared American cuisine during a break in the canteen. The entire process of sharing developed very naturally and with ease, without having to designate a set timetable as to when she could intervene during a lesson as our education system often requires us to do. Maggie did not need for us to give her permission to do activities with the children. She just did. Every time it was natural for her. And we gave her many opportunities and considered her a huge resource to help us grow.

We cannot ignore the human aspect of this cultural exchange and collaboration. The integration of American girls like Maggie into the classes has had a huge impact on the relationships built by the children. The children understand better what hospitality means. They realize the importance of learning a foreign language in order to communicate. They come to understand the attention that needs to be paid to others. They become aware of the fact that the class is a small community in which following and letting certain rules be known is necessary. Maggie taught us this and so much more!

The last aspect I would like to highlight is that of mind expansion. We do everything we can to teach our children that they are not the center of the world and this experience helps us show that Italy is not the center of the world either. By comparing cultures, school systems, dishes, traditions and everything else, we begin to realize that before judging we need to acknowledge and consider other points of view as well.

Note

1. Stefania Lancellotti and Camilla Giovanardi, 1st and 2nd Grade Teachers, Giacomo Leopardi Primary School, Instituto Comprensivo Modena.

CHAPTER FIFTEEN

So, How Is the Food?

BETHANY McLAUGHLIN DOAN[1]

"Good night!" My host father exclaimed every morning when he woke me up for school. When I think back to my time spent with the study abroad program, I remember the little things that still bring a smile to my face, like successfully explaining to my host father the difference between good night and good morning as used in America. When I decided to study abroad in Modena, Italy, I really did not know what I was getting myself into. By the end of May I found myself in a foreign country, crying, not wanting to say goodbye to a family that four weeks earlier had been complete strangers, to students who spoke a different language than me yet captured my heart in mere days, and to fellow study abroad members I had never seen before on the vast UGA campus and I never saw again, but played a significant role in creating the Italian memories that will last a lifetime. Although the focus of the program's experience is education in Italian schools, I came away from the trip with much more than something to add to my teaching resume. However, I do have to admit, it has always been a highlight and phenomenal talking point in job interviews throughout my career thus far.

The day to leave I arrived at the airport without any family or friends to wave me off as my family lives out of state and most of my friends at UGA had already rushed off for summer vacation. Stepping out of my comfort zone right away, I gathered with the other travelers I recognized from previous trip meetings as we awaited further instructions. Standing at the airport in the international security line with my new, blank passport ready for its first stamp, I was most concerned with thoughts like, "Did I pack enough"? "How much longer until I lose cell service"? "What if I don't end up with internet access as I was promised"? "Who will I sit by on the longest plane ride of my life"? Thoughts of safety, the language barrier, living situation challenges, or even teaching Italian middle school children, the focus of the trip, were the furthest things from my inexperienced mind.

Our group landed in Modena in a haze. Between the time change, my lengthy first international flight, and the built-up excitement and apprehension, my first few moments on the ground in Italy, with my new group of best friends who had bonded on the eight hour flight, are hard to recall. I attribute some of this blank memory space to the fact that thus far, we were a group. The other girls and I experienced everything together. We were companions through it all—the pre-departure planning sessions, the bus rides, the confines of our daunting first international flight, and navigating airports with little to no English being understood. We were a group of Americans in the same situation, with the same lack of experiences and naivetés, together for Maymester.

Until we weren't. Upon arrival in Modena, we became individual, anxious Americans as we separated and met our host families for the first time. Being able to communicate with my host family for weeks up until my arrival in Italy was the only reassurance I had that kept me from breaking down that first day. My host family was anxiously awaiting the arrival of our bus and could barely contain their excitement when we first met. However, once introductions were over, we were dismissed from the group of travelers, my comfort zone, the only sense of familiarity I had so far, and sent to live with our host Italian family for the rest of Maymester.

My first stop with my new host family after introductions and the initial excitement subsided—the gelatoria. Being an ice cream fanatic, to say I was excited would be an understatement, but my excitement at this point was undermined by my burning desire to run back to the bus and to anyone who spoke English. Much to my surprise, though, my first taste of pure, Italian gelato was all I could ever imagined it would be, and anxious smiles and prolonged smiles that came with it during my first day with my host family are also just as memorable.

We arrived at my new home that first day, with extra gelato in tow, and I was shown my borrowed bedroom—my host sister's regular room in her family's flat. As explained in meetings prior to the trip, most families live in apartment type flats. Homeownership is not as common as it is in America. My host sister, Fru, spoke the most English of the family since she was the oldest and further along in her schooling. In Italian schools, students are taught English beginning in elementary school, so it is common for most children to have more English language acquisition and experience with the language than parents. Luckily, my suitcase had not been lost (one of my initial fears), and I did in fact have Internet access at my new home. My worries were easing as I settled in and my first dinner with my new family began.

Pasta, bread, wine, pizza... and then more pizza. After everything I imagined Italian food to be, my expectations fell unbelievably short. Italian food is fresh, delicious, and plentiful. American versions of Italian food, whether in a restaurant or in a family kitchen, can never compare to the authenticity, taste, and indescribable quality of Italian food. One of the recommendations from former study abroad students was to keep a journal to remember time spent in Italy. My journal is heavily focused on my different food experiences and even contains wrappers to my favorite Italian delicacies to remember for my next return to Italy. To this day, I refuse to eat at Olive Garden. Once your taste buds are introduced to pure Italian food, be forewarned, you can never go back.

The first of many dinners with Google translate as the centerpiece of the table took place my first night in Modena, and I slowly but surely got to know the Italians whose roof I was sleeping under—a family who graciously welcomed me into their home for an entire month. The first night after dinner, I presented my family with a few typically American gifts to thank them for their generosity. Peanut butter was the biggest hit of all since it is not common in Italy. I later learned why this is. Nutella, a staple in Italian homes, is the preferred spreadable topping for anything you can imagine, and it prevails over the entire country. I can proudly attest to the fact that I had Nutella at every meal, at every time of the day, and in almost every imaginable way, shape, and form. The peanut butter for my family, though, was not seen as an equivalent to Nutella. It was deemed a treasured foreign delicacy that they were extremely grateful to receive, since they had never tasted this mysterious substance.

Everyone said before we embarked on the trip that we would soon refer to our host families as our actual family, and we would begin to call them as mom, dad, sister, and brother. This was very hard for me to believe. How in only a few short weeks could the strange people in a foreign land earn the same coveted titles I gave my family in America? This inclination, however, was one of the first realizations of the experience that I didn't see this coming. My *mom* lives in Italy with my *dad*, my *sister*, that I have always wanted, and my *brother*. To this day, thanks in part to social media, I still keep in touch with my sister and brother. Just recently I mailed them an invitation to my wedding, six years after my trip to Modena and our first meeting filled with awkward silences and uneasy smiles.

This experience, which I could talk about for hours on end, changed me immensely. It seems cliché to even say such a thing, but there really is no better way to attest to everything I saw, heard, and experienced in my short time in Modena. Studying abroad, this trip in particular, opened my eyes to the world, and

I don't just mean to a new language, a new area of the world, or even to teaching in a different country. My eyes were opened to differences. Differences that go beyond physical attributes to cultures, perceptions, and who I am as an individual.

To me the most notable difference between Italian culture and that of America is the Italian emphasis on the importance of family. The family bond has no bounds, no limit in Italy. Families go to extreme lengths just to spend lunch or dinner together. There are no phones during dinner, no distractions from conversations, and no unwillingness to spend quality time together. My host family and I sat around their porch table for hours, long after meals were over, discussing anything and everything that our language barrier allowed. My sister and brother were active in the conversations and family events, never once complaining of the time commitment or lost time with friends because of this strange American girl who had invaded their space. In comparison in America, often phones, TVs, or other distractions are not only used during mealtime but are the focus. Often, as soon as the actual eating of the meal is complete, family members disperse to separate rooms, tasks, or events, and significant family time is sacrificed. The Italian emphasis on family extends to all members not just to those under the same roof. My brother, sister, and I spent many lunches at our grandparents' house, as well.

One of these lunches happens to be one of my most memorable, forever known to me as the day I was tricked into eating horsemeat by my host family. *Tricked* sounds more menacing than it actually was. However, my family, aware of the fact that horse meat is not a regular food source or choice for Americans, were excited to see my reaction and eager to share an Italian custom with me. Once I had finished eating, without questioning the source of the beef-looking meat in my pasta (at this point, I ate any and all pasta without reservation, knowing it would be just as delicious as the one before), my sister, my most trusted translator now, informed me of the meat source as everyone burst out laughing. I can only imagine the shades of red my face became due to my embarrassment and surprise! We recalled this event for days to come. A harmless experiment turned into an unforgettable, laughable memory that bonded my family and me even more.

Another of the innumerable ways the trip changed me came in my realization of the power of perception and its many forms—my perception of others, their perception of me, and my self-perception. Simply put, I became more aware of the image and persona I was presenting to others. Without the use of a common language, I had to rely on nonverbal communication to convey my personality, my kindness, and my appreciation. I became more aware of my body language, my facial expressions, and the attitude I was portraying without the use of words to fall back on to clarify. Italians are much more in touch with nonverbal cues and communication than I believe Americans are. They hug more, show appreciation more openly, and are quick to smile even when it is out of confusion or as a result of a disconnect. I realized my need to be clear and concise with my intentions, to be understanding and patient, and to be open to anything and everything I encountered.

From spending afternoons at home with my host family, to weekly seminars, to weekend trips to Verona, Venice, and Florence, and sleepovers with my sister's friends, I was forced, apprehensively at first, into uncomfortable, new situations. However, these situations and time spent with new people made me more aware of myself, my actions, my thoughts, and my approach to life. This anxious American girl who wanted to run away on the first day in Modena was transformed into an honorary Italian in a short time, eager for new adventures, new cities, and new wonders of the world. Gone were my preconceived notions of Italy and Europe in general and replaced with experiences, memories (like meeting TV's Jersey Shore in a Venice pizza shop!), and friendships I will always treasure. Clichéd feelings of happiness, pure joy, and engagement replaced the naïveté I arrived with, and for that, I am forever grateful. I may not eat in Italian restaurants in America any longer after having tasted the pasta and gelato of the Promised Land, but I keep the lessons I learned and appreciation I gained with me still to this day as a teacher and as a more well-rounded, confident, and adventurous individual.

As a teacher now reflecting back, the experience illuminated the reality of differences among the students within my classroom. Not everyone comes from the same background, which we had been taught in education classes at UGA, but to see the differences in culture, in students, in families, firsthand, is an element of learning that cannot be replicated in America. Teaching in Modena, walking to school every day with the students of my middle school, sharing snack breaks with students in the hallways (because as a I mentioned, lunch is at home for families to come together), I saw the impact of one person. My students definitely did not always understand me and vice versa. However, we created connections stronger than a common language, overcoming our once terrifying differences.

My students in Modena were similar to those I had tutored or volunteered with in American schools at first glance, but they were entirely different at the same time. I saw commonalities as far as ability, respect, and an eagerness to learn, but I also saw differences in behavior, attitudes, and their approach to school as a whole. Students may have begrudgingly come to class some days during my month in Modena, but once they were there, they knew their purpose, they knew their goals, and they knew how they must act accordingly in order to teach them. I brought back to my student teaching and to my then future career in education their overwhelming attitudes of acceptance, patience, and forgiveness. Even though I speak the same language as most of my students in my American classroom, messages are sometimes misconstrued, complicated, or confusing. Just as I did with my Italian 6th graders, I approach my 12th grade seniors with the same open, all-encompassing concept of education. They know that I am always open to talk, open to listen, open to change, and open to help them beyond academics. I eat lunch with my students, talk with them in the hallways, and engage in their personal lives. At the base of successful teaching is a strong rapport. In order to learn and become involved as active participants in their own schooling, students need to feel received and appreciated, just as I was received and appreciated by my Modena school, my host family, and by the other study abroad members.

As I approach the end of my fourth full year of teaching high school English, having taught all grades 9–12 from remedial to advanced, I have a sense of accomplishment. Academically, I have instructed and aided in the creation of successful, productive students. Emotionally, I have been able to connect with students who previously never connected with anyone at school. Those students who dread coming to school each day, who feel alone, who question their purpose in the school and the world. I have built stronger and stronger rapports with my students, keeping in touch with them long after the completion of my class and graduation. While both academically and emotionally I feel successful as a teacher, I know I still have a message to spread and an eagerness to instill in my students the same drive, motivation, and energy to get out in the world and experience it that my students in Modena shared with me. I am reminded daily of the importance of nonverbal communication, the impact of differences, and the necessity to go above and beyond to help my students achieve their goals. Whether it be learning a second language or analyzing an American text, students across the world have the same universal needs: to be accepted, to be connected, and to be successful. Modena, Calvino Middle School, and my time exploring Italy was my first major stepping-stone to this vital component to successful teaching and mentoring.

I often talk of my time in Italy, reminiscing on silly memories like late nights in hostels, long, un-air-conditioned train rides, sweaty nights, unnerving amounts of pizza, pasta, gelato, and Nutella consumption, and I even still remember a handful of Italian phrases like, "Andiamo". I've talked about my time in Italy in job interviews, highlighting how I have tailored my educational philosophy and teaching practice as a result of it. I explain how the experience helped me grow as an educator, and how I have expanded my horizons as an individual. Most significantly though, I focus not on the past, but on my current actions and potential that result from my Maymester abroad. I have since taken over sixty students to various counties around the world during spring break study abroad programs, emphasizing to student the benefits they will reap from the travel through my own experiences studying abroad. I have travelled to London, Prague, Budapest, Germany, Ireland, Wales, and Hungary preaching the benefits of travel to students. The experiences force high schoolers into daunting situations that test their morals, principles, and strengths. My trips have helped me give back the experience that first started my motivation to explore the world, to widen my horizons, and to become a better-rounded, appreciative American. My students return from these trips with a new sense of being, a new appreciation for their lives and relationships, and a broader acceptance of differences.

I pride myself on the fact that I am continuing my passion for exploration and knowledge with my students—the students who rarely pry their eyes off their cell phones, who only know one house, one neighborhood, and one set of friends. Traveling to areas with no cell service, and no Google at their fingertips for reference and information, my students are tested and tested again on these journeys. However, they grow immeasurably in a short time, just as I did in Modena, as they glimpse the power of travel and return year after year for another trip.

Not only do I travel with students to international locations, but I have since been traveling, backpacking, and immersing myself in cultures on my own accord, as well. Italy became the beginning of my true appreciation of life, differences, and unique cultures. Modena was the starting point for my knowledge and adventure seeking. From Paris to Rome to Italy (two more times) to Amsterdam and Spain, my drive to see more, know more, and do more has only increased as I add stamps to my once empty passport. No longer do I have petty worries when boarding the (still daunting) long international flights. Instead, I am filled with anticipation, excitement, and yearning for all that is to come, lost luggage and internet connection or not. My next stop? Thailand. My final stop? Still to be determined as my growth, knowledge, awareness, understanding, and appreciation for others, my students, and new experiences continue to expand, and I strive for more. Until then, "Ciao" as the Italians say, or "Good morning" as my father said each night before bed when I was fortunate enough to spend a few weeks under the roof of these amazing people who entered my life as complete strangers.

Note

1. Bethany McLaughlin Doan, 10th and 12th Grade Teacher, Chesterfield County (Virginia) Public Schools.

CHAPTER SIXTEEN

Double the Pleasure

RACHEL MILLER McKEE[1]

Four years ago my life changed forever. Four years ago, at the age of 23, I flew for the very first time. Growing up, my parents never travelled but I always had such an itch to travel and see the sights. I wanted to do a study abroad while in college but it just never worked out. While in my master's program, I heard something about a trip to Italy. I instantly made it my life mission to go on this trip and just hoped that somehow I could get class credit that counted towards my program and that there were still openings available. I was in luck all the way around!

That was four years ago. Because of my experience, I returned to Italy three summers in a row. I would have returned for a 4th summer, but chose, instead, to get married. Throughout this experience, I was able to not just have one host family, but two incredible host families that changed my life and welcomed me with open arms. The first two summers I lived with the sweetest family ever-the Fanelli's. The third summer my family was unable to host me so I was placed with another family. I was so sad that I wasn't able to be with the Fanelli's! I couldn't imagine being with another family! As it turns out, I ended up loving my second family, the Rinaldi's, just as much. Patrizia, her daughter Eugenia, and her parents instantly made me a part of their family. I still got to see and spend some time with the Fanelli's too. Now, not only did I have one incredible Italian family, I had two. I quickly realized that it was going to break my heart to leave the Rinaldi's just like it did each time I left the Fanelli's. I am truly blessed to have had the chance to live with both of these families. They went out of their way to let a stranger into their homes and instantly and unconditionally made me a part of their families.

Prior to leaving America that first time I was beyond excited but also very nervous! I will never forget the first time I got an email from my host family complete with a photograph and information about them. I could not wait to meet them. I will also never forget the first time I laid eyes on my first host family, the Fanelli's. All of the UGA students were on a bus transporting us from Milan to Modena. The bus pulled into a parking lot where all of the Italian host families were awaiting our arrival. I could barely get off the bus I was so full of anxiety. I knew that my life was about to be forever changed. I remember seeing my host family and being so excited to meet them! In the car ride to their apartment I quickly realized how little Italian I knew, aka none, and that communication was going to be very challenging. Luckily, my host family was very patient with me, and I taught them lots of English while they taught me some Italian. One of the biggest realizations I had while there was how small a part language plays in communication. Oral language is not required in order to form bonds that will last a lifetime.

My host families became everything to me. I have never felt so welcomed and included in my entire life. They made me a part of their families. They will never know how much they have truly impacted me and how much they mean to me. During my second time there I remember a car ride home after the Fanelli's took me to visit Lake Garda, which is hands down the most beautiful lake I have ever seen. During that ride back I had silent tears running down my face in the back seat because I was just so thankful and loved my family so much. I could not, and still cannot believe how blessed I was to have been taken in by such remarkable people. There were so many special moments, like every time Emilia or Eugenia would grab my hand when we were walking. Or when Fabio and I would constantly pick at each other. Or the real-life talks Patrizia and I had about the world. Or all of the times sitting at the dinner table talking with Pietro and Angelica. They have no idea how special every single moment was to me.

The culture there is like nothing I had ever experienced before. Everyone and everything is just so relaxed. Bikes are a common mode of transportation. A favorite part of my days was casually riding my bike to my school to be with my kindergartners or to get to the summer camp. It was just so different from home where I always feel pressured and late and trying to get everywhere in my car. There, I would have a breakfast of cookies and cappuccino and then go hop on my bike for my peaceful ride. I discovered what a pleasant way that was to start a day. That feeling of no stress and no rushing was addicting. I often find myself saying, "I just want to be in Italy." There is a peace in your soul there that can only be understood when it is experienced.

Modena is one of the most beautiful towns I have ever seen. I love the down-town area with the cobblestone streets. I took every opportunity to ride my bike down those streets just looking around and taking in all the amazing scenery. Some of the other girls from the group and I had a favorite wine café in the "centro" where we often met to talk about the incredible things we had seen and our experiences in our schools and with our families! I also developed a love for gelato. Comparing to it ice cream does not do it justice. My family joked with me constantly about my unwavering love for their gelato.

I will forever be grateful for all of the places and experience my families made possible for me. When I told them I had always dreamed of visiting Cinque Terre, they arranged a trip there. Both families took me to so many incredible places that I could have never even imagined visiting. Some of my favorites were the experiences only known by the locals like festivals, ancient castles, and old, beautiful towns.

A favorite night with the Fanelli's was making homemade gnocchini at the home of some of their friends. They explained that gnocchini meant "little ears" because of how it looks. It was truly an authentic experience to make it from scratch and, of course, it was delicious. A favorite cooking experiences with Patrizia and Eugenia was making homemade piadinas, delicious crunchy sand-wiches with prosciutto and a spread similar to mayonnaise.

My favorite meal in Italy happened in the mountains not too far from Modena. Patrizia's parents had a cabin in the mountains. During a visit there Patrizia's mother made lasagna for lunch. It doesn't get more authentic than home-made lasagna made by an Italian nona. It was hands down the best Italian food, or maybe any food, I have ever eaten. On the return home, Patrizia took Eugenia and me to a beautiful mountain town to take in its spectacular and breathtaking views. I decided that day that everywhere in Italy is spectacular. Every new place I laid my eyes on while there was just as gorgeous, or more jaw dropping than the one before.

Completely consumed by the beauty and kindness I had experienced in Italy, my boyfriend and I returned the following summer as graduation gifts to ourselves. We visited Rome, Pisa, Venice, Sorrento, Capri, Cinque Terre, and even London and Paris! It was the trip of a lifetime. We ended our travels in Modena where I was going to stay and work at the English summer camp organized by Victoria Language. The Fanelli's welcomed Jack with open arms, just like they had me. It was so special to me for him to get to meet them and see how truly wonderful this family was. I was finally having my two worlds meet!

I sent wedding invitations to both of my Italian families. I knew it was unlikely that they could attend, but I wanted them to know that I loved them and was thinking about them during this special time in my life. Surprisingly, I got a message from Patrizia confirming that she and Eugenia were in fact going to fly all the way to America and be there for our wedding! After receiving this unexpected news I literally sat on my couch and cried tears of joy. It was unbelievable that one of my Italian families would be there on my wedding day. They were able to fly in a few days before the wedding so I was able to give them a few experiences close to Athens and then they went on to visit another student they had hosted before taking in the sights in Miami and New York. Having them at my wedding was beyond touching. Their efforts solidified my thoughts that they, too, were my family.

The way I interact and plan for my ESOL students was greatly impacted by my time in Italy. I know that language can be a barrier, but there are many ways around it. I am convinced that I am a better-rounded educator because of my experiences there. I also always try to take into account the pressures that my students face here and the emphasis on creativity and 'no wrong answer' there. I try to give my students chances to express themselves and be creative without fear of humiliation like I observed in the schools in Italy. Visiting the different schools there was eye-opening and offered valuable strategies and activities to bring home to my own classroom. I was amazed at the amount and quality of child created art. The overall development and well-being of children was an obvious focus for the schools with little emphasis on test scores. Creativity literally oozed out of the schools. As a teacher I found it refreshing and inspiring!

The study abroad program provided me a life changing experience. Through this experience a fire was lit inside of me. My life goal is to travel and take part in new cultural experiences every chance that I can. It should be a college requirement for every student to take a trip such as this, make a connection with a foreign family, and have their eyes opened to the world around them before entering the "work world". I am truly blessed to have been a part of this program, to have gotten to know and be influenced by Dr. Tolley and Roberta and the rest of the Victoria Language team, to see and experience so many incredible things, and to have joined two amazing Italian families that will forever hold a special place in my heart.

Note

1. Rachel Miller McKee, 2nd Grade Teacher, Clarke County (Georgia) School District.

PART FIVE

Subtleties

A cultural exchange experience holds anticipation of big surprises and life changing opportunities. Often, the anticipation paints an unrealistic picture that can cloud our vision and leave us with preconceived notions and expectations. We spend months preparing for the adventure and in those months conjure up images of a new life, family, and routine, dismissing the idea that it is only to be a temporary arrangement. The glamour and romanticism of our suppositions consume us. Each day our imaginations lead us to believe that all Italians live in beautiful villas, that all Americans have traveled extensively throughout the USA, and that the soon-to-be-experienced encounters and adventures will be accompanied by whistles and bells. Demchuk (2014) warns "don't be a victim to the 'expectations vs. realities' syndrome that can dampen your time studying abroad. It's one of the few experiences in life that can really live up to its hype … and don't expect every day to feel like the final scene in a movie (although some will)!" (p. 1). When the day arrives and new families meet and unite for the first time and Italian and soon-to-be American teachers come face-to-face in the Italian classrooms, the glitter can fade and hints of disillusionment begin to dull the once perceived glamour. Some are left wondering what happened. Where is the magic that they expected to find? In the months of anticipation there were never thoughts of frustration and confusion.

The days of self-doubt and self-questioning come and go, and in the midst of the confusion when least expected the clouds part. The confused are heartened by impromptu laughter, softened by the smile of a child who finally understands a message, touched by the simple gesture of a homemade meal, and warmed by acts of human kindness and understanding that transcend cultures and need no translation. These subtle awakenings come without the anticipated whistles and bells, but leave resounding impressions. Both American students and Italian hosts are blindsided by these subtleties … true instances of not seeing the forests for the trees. They look for and expect fireworks. The subtle impacts were something they didn't see coming.

There are unexpected opportunities for reflecting on how they perceive language and behaviors and how others do the same. The subtle lessons of remembering to think before speaking and acting offer opportunities for putting themselves in the shoes of others. There is also the very subtle and unexpected realization that they are immersed in an academic program in which academics are overshadowed by just experiencing things and taking it all in (Hopkins, 1999). They learn to live the clichés of smelling the roses, appreciating the journey as much as the destination, and literally doing as the Romans do (Hopkins, 1999). These commonsense guidelines of everyday life suddenly take on much more subtle but meaningful interpretation when immersed in unknown terrain and circumstances. Instead of being knocked off their feet as anticipated by boisterous adventures and expected confusion and chaos, they are instead rocked by warm, quiet smiles, a magical moment frozen in time during a family car trip, children's reactions to American teachers, and the plethora of personalities and qualities of American students.

The Corciolani family, who has hosted seven students during the nine years of the program, Sara, Natalia, and Concetta offer stories that attest to the subtleties that they never saw coming. Their stories remind us that we often try too hard to make things happen or anticipate all that might go wrong, instead of just letting things happen naturally. This message certainly rings true with Natalia who returned the year following her participation to serve as a student helper and found herself in Pisa, entering the Duomo for mass, and being asked by the priest to read scriptures for the English mass that was about to take place. I remember her telling me of this experience and remarking that she was literally shaking. Certainly it was an opportunity that she never saw coming but will remember for the rest of her life.

References

Demchuk, A. (2014). *Studying abroad: Expectations vs. reality?* Retrieved from https://www.goabroad.com/articles/study-abroad/studying-abroad-expectations-vs-reality

Hopkins, J. R. (1999). Studying abroad as a form of experiential education. *Liberal Education, 85*(3), 36–45.

CHAPTER SEVENTEEN

The Longevity Award

THE CORCIOLANI FAMILY (ELENA, LAURA, PIERO)[1]

We are the Corciolani family: Elena, Laura, and Piero! We have been participating in the UGA/Modena Schools Project since its beginning in 2009, and we have hosted seven girls. Thanks to this experience, we have grown and been influenced from a cultural, linguistic, and also human point of view. We have had opportunities to compare ourselves to ideas, habits, and cuisines that are different from ours, and this has given us so much in return. Each student has offered a unique experience for our family. We have learned something from each of them, and the experience has always been so delightful.

We will always treasure the shyness of the first days together, the smiles, the gestures, the chats, the jokes, and the continuous laughter that we shared with each of the girls we have had the pleasure to host! Abby, Sara, Mary Katherine, Shaquila, Chelsea, Heather, and Marisa – each of them has given us a bit of herself and a bit of cheerfulness. Despite the distance that separates us, they will always be part of our family! We are forever grateful to Victoria Language for offering us inclusion in this amazing program and say "THANK YOU VICTORIA LANGUAGE AND UGA" for allowing us to live this remarkable experience!

Note

1. Corciolani Family (Elena, Laura, and Piero), Italy Host Family.

CHAPTER EIGHTEEN

Challenge Accepted

SARA LORENZINI[1]

One of my big limits and one that I believe is also my largest cultural gap is that I have never studied English despite the many years I have spent on books! Welcoming into my classes, over the years, American students who knew little to nothing about the Italian language has been, first and foremost, a challenge to myself and to my pupils who surely know the language way better than me.

Now, I can say that I have accepted that challenge. I have always established good relationships with the girls who have attended my classes. These relationships were built on empathy, mutual acceptance, and a desire to put myself in the game and experience everything possible with the students who, in turn, have had the opportunity to come in touch with different people who have surely enriched them both on the cultural and the human level.

In particular, I want to recall two moments of our hosting the American students. The first was in May a few years ago, the year of the disastrous earthquake that struck Modena. The morning of one of the largest shocks, my American student was in class with me and we were doing an activity on the names of the fruits and their characteristics. The shake caught everyone by surprise. Even though there had been foreshocks, no one could have imagined what was about to happen.

The children looked at me, the American student was breathless, the alarm was ringing … a collection of agitated moments. At first everyone hid under the desks and then, once the shake had ended, ran out as fast as possible. Once we were in the street, I realized that the American student had gone pale and was very frightened. At that moment we did not need words, neither Italian nor English ones. We understood each other perfectly with just one glance. Then, a very nice thing happened. The children started asking her how she was and were happy to cheer her up. In the following days our school was closed because of the shocks that went on for a long time. Unfortunately, neither the children nor I had the occasion to thank her and tell her goodbye. For this we were very sad.

The second moment I recall goes back a few years after that. I was teaching second grade, and we were supposed to visit a farm on the hills, not far from Modena, for our orchard project. It had rained a lot in the previous days and the temperature, although it was May, was quite cold. The American student came to school in the morning with a short skirt, a t-shirt, and sandals! That is what we call beachwear, I thought to myself.

I was a little puzzled. I wondered if maybe I had not been clear enough about our plan and where we were going. Regardless, we visited the farm, the garden, and the orchard. In a few spots the ground was quite muddy. The kids started to play sliding down a hill and, instead of complaining about not having worn the right outfit, the girl joined in and played with them. When we returned to school we were all tired, happy, and very dirty, but she was way more tired than we were and even happier. Who knows what she thought about the Italian teachers bringing their students to a muddy field. However, in the end, using gestures, few words and body language we agreed it was worth it. I was made aware of the flexibility and the willingness to be a part of our class activities of our American guest.

All this to say, that despite my limited linguistic skills, and the fact that my English has not improved a lot over the years, I would welcome one of these fantastic girls tomorrow because, with their curiosity and desire to get to know and understand us, they are always a breath of fresh air. We always find ways to understand each other, one way or another.

Note

1. Sara Lorenzini, 3rd Grade Teacher, Emilio Po Elementary School.

CHAPTER NINETEEN

Things Come in Threes

NATALIA PRADA-REY COOPER[1]

Traveling. It leaves you speechless then turns you into a storyteller. I have never claimed to be much of a storyteller, but there is one story I do love to tell. And that is of my journey to Italia, and its profound impact on my life.

My story begins in the freshman dorms at The University of Georgia where I spent hours researching study abroad programs. Staying up late, dreaming about adventures in Austria, Australia, and even Antarctica was a common habit. As an education major, I knew I wanted an experience that would add to my repertoire as a future educator. When the education program in Italy finally caught my eye, I felt like I had won the lottery! This was exactly what I was searching for. I (impatiently and eagerly) waited to apply until my junior year of college. After two years of researching and dreaming, I would leave on May 9, 2009.

The meetings leading up to the trip are fond and vivid memories. I remember sitting at an oval table, looking around at the other participants, none of whom I knew, and wondering if they shared my feelings of excitement. International travel has been a constant in my life. My parents are from Peru and Colombia, so I have had a passport since I was a baby. For several of my peers this was their first time to leave the country. Their concerns were "What time should we arrive at the airport"? "How will my body react to the jetlag"? "Is traveling to Italy safe"? "Can we drink the water there"? While these were extremely valid and relevant concerns when traveling overseas for thirty days, all I wanted to know was, "When do we meet our families?" "How will we be matched with our classrooms?" "Do we get to learn Italian?" and, of course, "How do I schedule a wine tour?"

Eventually, all my questions were addressed and all that did was add to my excitement. A family would welcome me into their home in a 'suburb' of Modena, Italy. This family consisted of a father (a truck driver), a mother (an accountant), a daughter (a middle schooler), a son (an elementary school student), and a toddler son. It would be a great match! I would be working in a first grade classroom and that suited me perfectly! We had an Italian teacher attend a few of our pre-departure meetings and teach us some useful Italian vocabulary. This was especially exciting to me because I am fluent in Spanish and a student of French. Learning Italian made it much more real. And, finally, came the answer to my vino question. There would be an optional excursion during our weekend in Florence. We would drive to a Tuscan villa where we would spend the day cooking fresh pasta and tasting Chianti wine. I was already speechless, and it was only January!

Departure day finally arrived, and I felt prepared but nervous. Not only was I about to spend a Maymester in Italy, but after studying abroad I was to meet my friend in Rome and continue traveling throughout Europe for another month. I put on my bravest face and said my goodbyes to my family in the Hartsfield-Jackson International Airport. On my way to meet the group at our gate, I walked briskly to the women's restroom, located an empty stall, locked the door, and started sobbing. Fear overtook whatever common sense I had left. "Get it together!" I thought to myself. "You've been waiting for this since 2006 in the Creswell dorms. This is your dream come true! Why are you crying?" I don't know if it was the fact that the next day was Mother's Day and it would be the first one spent without my mom, or the fact that I was about to be 4,860 miles away from home, but I was sick to my stomach with nerves. After some deep breaths and several splashes of water to my face, I made my way to the gate with a smile on my face. As soon as I was reunited with the group, the nerves faded. It turned out everyone felt the same way. Some were still red-faced from the tears they had shed in the terminal. We talked about our expectations for the trip ahead.

After boarding the flight, my nerves eased but kept trying to make an unwelcomed return. Sleep was hard to come by on that nine hour flight to Milan. We landed in Italy, made our way through customs and found our carousel at baggage claim. My oversized bag had made it safely! All I wanted to do was call my mom and tell her we had arrived and that everyone's accents were even more charming than anticipated. From Milan, we had another leg of our journey to complete. We boarded a bus that would transport our group from the airport to the Modena bus station. My observations from the bus were that not much was different. The cars had different license plates. The weather was a little cooler. Otherwise, I just felt a little groggy and delusional. I nodded off from time to time, but the excitement fed my adrenaline.

Once we arrived at the bus station, the exchange happened very quickly. It was a total blur. I was introduced to my family. I got into their car and began to realize something when I spoke in English. My thoughts were—"Wait. They don't seem to understand me … OK. Let me try Spanish … OK. Now they *really* don't know what I am saying … OK. Just nod and smile and listen. Try to pick out familiar words." And so, that is what I did. That Sunday, we got gelato and went to a park located right behind their home. We took a walk while making many failed attempts to communicate. Frustration, due to my lack of ability to communicate and, certainly, lack of sleep began to creep up inside me. I passed it off as jetlag. During our afternoon stroll, we ran into one of my peers. She was with her family and, to my surprise, I noticed they were successfully communicating in English! Why, I wondered, was I paired with a family who did not seem to understand English? Following my feelings of frustration came isolation. When my family would all laugh at something, I missed the humor. At dinner that night I felt defeated. I could not join the conversation, yet I had so many questions! I wanted to share my life story and hear theirs. Yes, the fresh pasta, topped with tuna and ripe tomato sauce, paired with a soothing wine was a nice distractor, but I could not imagine living in this darkness for another twenty-nine days.

My first day in my Italian classroom began with a chaotic morning at home. They were a family of five going about their daily lives with large amounts of Italian banter adjusting to a stranger who had burst their bubble of normalcy and made them a family of 5+1. Arriving at my school, I walked into the classroom and saw two adults. The students were participating in whole-class drills, and the teachers were strict when a student spoke out of turn. When I introduced myself, some familiar feelings arose—frustration, isolation, and defeat. They didn't understand me either. So, not only was I living with a family who didn't understand me, but I was also expected to implement lessons in an environment where the teachers wouldn't understand me. I had expected that the students would not speak English, but I was taken aback when I discovered the same about the teachers. At least the bambini were adorable! I wanted to cry. All this build-up, countless hours spent researching, packing, planning, and preparing and I could see no silver lining. At least, not yet.

As the jetlag wore off and the connections with my fellow study abroad participants deepened, I realized we were all in uncharted territory together. We were tired, disoriented, and experiencing culture shock. There were a lot of unknowns. I was in a new city, living with a new family, grappling with a new language, working in a new school, visiting a new country, and living on a new continent. And each of those spaces had its own way of functioning, all of which were foreign to me.

The shift eventually happened. I could sense that silver lining in the distance. I'm not sure of the exact moment. Looking back, I recall three moments that stand out in my mind that made me think – I've made it. I love it here. This place will forever be a part of me. These people are my family. These were the moments that I never saw coming.

One of these moments occurred around the dinner table. The same dinner table where those most uncomfortable moments took place on my first night in Italy. Six nights later laughter brought me to tears during dinner with my famiglia. The topic of conversation is a blur, but I do remember that something was lost in translation, and it made us all laugh so hard. On that first day, I wasn't laughing with them. But in this moment, when I joined in their laughter, I felt connected. I was enriched. I was reminded of why I had lost sleep researching study abroad programs in the first place. It was for this feeling. This was my family. I am almost brought to tears just putting these words in writing and reliving this joyous memory. In my journal, I wrote how I felt like they were truly my family. That night, I was speechless.

The second ah-ha moment happened after school one day. I had quickly fallen into a routine. Mia mamma would take me to school, I would teach lessons to my first graders, and then I would go to Nonna's (grandma's) house. There I would eat lunch and rest before our afternoon seminars or excursions. Nonna spoke no English and I no Italian. Yet, somehow, magically, we communicated. She would tell me stories and I would listen enthusiastically. One particular day she had made fresh gnocchi. She had hand-rolled the homemade potato dough into perfectly sized little balls. The smell of the apartment that day is unforgettable, and I am often transported back to that moment. The pride in her face when she served me that meal will live with me forever. It left me speechless. I was aware of the generosity of the Italian culture and realized how important it was to her to make me happy.

The third moment came during one of the last days with my famiglia. This was an emotionally fueled day. That evening all of the study abroad participants, their host families and teachers were to gather at the Modena Country Club to celebrate the end of a wonderful four weeks together. My humble father had never been to the country club and there was no GPS in the car. We were six passengers in a 5-person vehicle with one in a car seat with no idea of where we were going. We were crowded, sad, grumpy, and melting in the Italian summer heat! As expected the anticipated bickering began, and it was quite the scene! The hairpin turn down a country road caused us to bump into one another. The scene was gloomy at best. Magically, something happened. Papa started laughing. As soon as he did, mamma joined in and the kids followed suit. I recall laughing so hard at this moment and thinking to myself let this be a lesson: never take life too seriously. I think back fondly on that car ride. I've told and retold this story so many times. Yes, we were late to the party, but we made it. And we were all crying happy tears right up until the end of that special night. We were family, and that was all that mattered.

My experience in Italy is one of bliss. Working with the first grade children and teaching them was unforgettable. Watching them play Red Rover in their broken English and then collapse to the ground in fits of laughter brought so much joy to my pre-service teacher's heart. I realized that oral language was not necessary for us to communicate with each other. And I realized that I would take back to my American classroom experiences a new perspective of the challenges faced by non-English speaking children.

Traveling to Florence and Venice on weekend excursions, I discovered a side of myself that I had never known before. I felt myself being transformed into a global citizen. In my journal, I reflected how my fellow study abroad participants carefully planned each step of their day. Hesitant to plan every minute, I ventured off to explore on my own. I felt this would be good practice for my upcoming four weeks of continued travel through Europe. I loved exploring the dreamy Italian landscape! I absorbed all that there was to see and do and was beyond ecstatic when I was asked to participate with the 2010 group as a teaching assistant. This was an opportunity to assume responsibility and to share with the participants what they could expect from their time in Modena. My host family was thrilled that I was returning, and welcomed me with open arms. Returning to Italy felt like going home.

Six years later, I planned a trip to Europe with my husband, and of course, Italy was on our itinerary. After exchanging several messages with my host family, they met us in Cinque Terre on a Tuesday afternoon. We shared vino bianco and a bountiful platter of fresh seafood as the waves crashed on the coast of Vernazza. The laughter continued, just as it had on that memorable evening in June 2009. They dropped us off in Florence that evening, and I was aware that their genuine outpouring of hospitality and love for me was stronger than ever.

My story ends the same as it began. I still spend hours upon hours researching life-changing journeys. My experiences in Italy made me even more enthralled to see the rest of the world. New cultures, new people, and the boundless beauty continue to leave me speechless. Travel has opened my eyes to a great big world and to life lessons. And now, it has turned me into a storyteller.

Note

1. Natalia Prada-Rey Cooper, Educational Consultant, Peabody College.

CHAPTER TWENTY

Connecting Distant Worlds

CONCETTA PONTICELLI[1]

For five years the students of the University of Georgia have entered the Cavour Middle School classrooms bringing their enthusiasm and their desire to know our school system and our students, and in return they have received the same curiosity, warmth, and affection. May's appointment with the students of the University of Georgia is a time that our students cannot wait for and that connects two distant worlds through the desire to meet and communicate with each other. It is an experience that enriches everyone and shows how teaching and learning do not pass only through words, but also through the heart.

In 2016, *Giovanni XXIII* primary school was involved in the UGA/Modena Schools Project for the first time. With this program a university student is hosted in an Italian classroom. The second grade class selected consisted of twenty students, three of whom were followed by a special needs teacher, some with foreign parents, thus bilingual, and two little girls who had just arrived in Italy who did not speak fluent Italian. In the classroom there were four teachers—the teacher of Italian and English; the teacher of History, Geography, and Music with excellent English; the teacher of Mathematics, Science, Technology, Physical Education, and Arts who did not know English very well; and the special needs teacher who was present every morning during the activities and could translate when needed. Although some of the teachers did not speak English very well, it was interesting to experience the use of the foreign language in situations involving the American student actively while she was, in turn, observing the teaching and learning process in our school.

If I have to summarize this project in one word, then it would surely have to be exciting! Indeed, it was very exciting getting ready and preparing for this experience with the children, who were electrified and curious for such an important event. We welcomed our student, Katie, organizing a special welcome party, with both Italian and American flags in hands and hanging on the walls, a warm "Welcome" poster, and a snack with local products. It was also exciting for her to let us learn more about herself and her culture, sharing lessons, playing games, songs, listening to her readings, and collaborating to create simple English-language books. Obviously, not all the teachers were able to engage her completely due to the lesson topics that they were teaching at that particular moment. Indeed, during Mathematics, Science, History, and Geography, Katie did not participate actively. She stuck to watching and listening. However, she was much more involved when the students had to carry out various activities of writing, calculating, drawing and coloring, and during those moments, Katie went around the desks to observe and interact. Children often called her attention spontaneously to show her their work on their notebooks, to ask for help at calculation procedures, and simply to translate a word into English.

She also participated in the Italian intensive course activities when we pulled a small group out of the class to allow them to boost their Italian language skills. Katie and the children did simple exercises where they had to re-arrange some sentences. The group was made up children with difficulties as well and we noticed that they felt just as involved as their classmates and, in addition, they often felt like they were the protagonists of the lesson. In our opinion, it is essential that all the students feel involved in the lesson and for this reason this moment was very important.

Katie created a good relationship with the children who were also happy to relate to a new figure within the classroom, so much that she can really be considered one of their teachers. In addition to the curricular activities, we showed her the electronic attendance register, the children's diaries, and other school spaces where several projects had been done. Also, she had the opportunity to attend lessons in other classes in order to have a bigger and clearer picture.

At the end of this experience we can surely say that opening up to this exchange opportunity helps pupils deal with new opportunities that prepare for the great variety of situations that life offers daily. It was exciting to share simple routine moments with a special guest who gave them more values every single time she was with them. Finally, I use the words thank you to thank all those who allowed this to happen.

Note

1. Concetta Ponticelli, Principal, Comprehensivo Modena 1.

Collaboration

In the months prior to the American students arriving in Italy, Italian teachers prepare their children for the experience and communicate with their assigned University of Georgia students in order to offer ideas for class themes and related activities. They anticipate their role will be one of host to the American students and one of facilitating a setting in which the UGA students can explore and interact. They, like the UGA students, are apprehensive. Their conscientiousness pushes them to prepare for the best experience possible and offer a huge Italian welcome to the students. They create and wave American flags. The children prepare and display welcome posters. Children practice presentations and look forward to welcoming and then showing off for their long-anticipated "mother tongue" teachers. As the weeks approach, they prepare as if expecting houseguests.

Once the American students arrive and are in place in the classrooms, an unexpected facet of this hosting opportunity—the richness of collaboration—becomes known. Administrators and teachers are taken by surprise by the natural inclination to work and plan together. Like the American students, they begin to realize that oral language is not a vital component for planning meaningful activities and experiences for children and interacting with them. They begin to understand that teaching has its own unique language that transcends cultural boundaries. All involved become a team focused on what is best for children and how to best enhance their learning experiences. This opportunity, initially viewed as a commitment to open their schools and classrooms and provide an educational setting for young American visitors, becomes multi-faceted and reciprocal … something they didn't see coming. Zhao et al (2009) found that the collaborative efforts of students in an overseas teaching experience in China "had a notable impact on the participants in terms of their understanding of a different culture and ways of working with non-English speaking students" (p. 302). Efforts to work together in planning meaningful opportunities for the Italian children and navigating the day-to-day activities of host families, transcend into unexpected respect and admiration between American student and host families and teachers. These collaborative efforts help all involved learn more about themselves, different cultures, the universal characteristics of children and people in general, and enhance their problem solving skills. Gemignani (2009) found in study abroad programs "where students developed a strong connection to people in another country, there was a particularly powerful motivation toward increased understanding through a bond that was intellectual and emotional" (p. 184).

The chapters that follow clearly illustrate this bond that was formed between the American students, their Italian host families, and their Italian host teachers. They reverberate the idea that study abroad opportunities involving collaboration among cultures and with those from different backgrounds can significantly bring about and impact a reduction of prejudice and ethnocentrism resulting in greater cultural understanding and global citizenship (Pettigrew & Tropp, 2000). McMillan and Opem (2005) share findings that collaborative efforts and powerful impressions from host countries result in return trips to and continued communication between host families. This is certainly the case with many of the students and host families from the UGA/Modena Schools Program.

Davide, Elsa, Anna, Francesca, Ivana, Roberta and Anna highlight the collaboration that has resulted from the UGA/Modena Schools program. Each year the collaboration grows stronger. All have been involved with the program for most, if not all, of the years of its existence, and the collaborative efforts to improve and expand upon the program are vital to its success and longevity. The richness of the collaborations result in increased learning opportunities for the American students and the Italian families and teachers. My collaboration with Roberta and Anna and the Victoria Language associates surpasses most of my working relationships with UGA colleagues. Our commitment to the program, the students, the families, and the teachers, and the Italian children pushes us to plan effectively, meaningfully, and wisely in order for all to benefit at a high level. As we approach the planning for year #10 we have taken a step back and reflected on the richness of the collaborations that we never saw coming and strive to continue the educational and cultural rigor of what is already in place.

References

Gemignani, C. L. (2009). *Understanding the study abroad experience of university students* (Graduate thesis dissertation, Iowa State University). Retrieved from http://lib.dr.iastate.edu/etd/10624

McMillan, A. R., & Opem, G. (2005). *Study abroad: A lifetime of benefits.* Retrieved from https://www.iesabroad.org/study-abroad/news/study-abroad-lifetime-benefits

Pettigrew, T. F., & Tropp, L. R. (2000). Does intergroup contact reduce prejudice? Recent meta-analytic findings. In S. Oskamp (Ed.), *Reducing prejudice and discrimination*, 93–114. Mahwah, NJ: Lawrence Erlbaum.

Zhao, Y., Meyers, L., & Meyers, B. (2009). Cross-cultural immersion in China: Preparing pre-service elementary teachers to work with diverse student populations in the United States. *Asia-Pacific Journal of Teacher Education, 37*(3), 295–317.

CHAPTER TWENTY-ONE

It's No Act

DAVIDE VERNIA[1]

I met the UGA/Modena Schools project delegation for the first time during the school year 2009 when the group came to visit the *Childhood Centre, MoMo*, where I was working. MoMo is an experiential and educational center located in the heart of Modena that welcomes boys and girls from 1 to 11 years old and provides nursery (years 0 to 3), Game Centre (years 2 to 5), and Laboratories (years 6 to 11) services to children and families. My experience with the UGA students has continued at the pre-school and kindergarten to which I moved in the school year 2012–13.

These two scholastic and educational structures are quite different from each other, but they are characterized by these key elements: (a) children; (b) teachers; (c) relationships; (d) past and future experiences; (e) planning; and (f) school routine. During each visit with the UGA students, I sensed that both the students and their professors are very interested in these key elements and look at them with attention and sensitivity.

What struck me the most was their ability to enter the educational contexts with a careful and thoughtful look, observing and listening to the situations explained by the teachers with respect, and, above all, their willingness to compare realities and educational styles different from theirs (the Italian school system, the Modena district one in particular, and the American one), finding in our realities the opportunity to grasp ideas and elements of comparison and reflection. These reflections arise from the fact that these types of schools are associated with the idea of a school tailor-made for children and teachers, a school open to everyone, a school that can offer educational opportunities to everyone, taking into account the singularities of each person. A school that values diversities and cultures, and yet, a school that everyone helps build, where the resources of the individual become wealth for the community, where learning with others is a unique and enriching source for children, teachers, administrators, and parents.

I could also see myself in their ways of approaching the children and community with them, using thoughtfulness together with the abilities to start with them an interesting dialogue that helps in building mutual knowledge and bases the future relationship on mutual trust.

Of course, the American language, despite being unknown to the children, has never been an obstacle to communication among the American students, our teachers, and our children. It is important to understand how having common ground to stand upon can be a successful way to break barriers and have both parties reflect on their points of view.

Our teachers' responsibilities, knowing about the arrival of the UGA delegations, has always addressed the need to speak early to the children of their visit, having them get involved in the realization of everything that could favor and enhance the reception; and the children have always been enthusiastic about it. This enthusiastic attitude has always met with the American students' indisputable appreciation and gratitude. This also allowed an important encounter between two realities, so that one met the other in a context of mutual availability, where reception was perceived as a strong and important experience of growth and evolution at both personal and collective levels.

Whenever a delegation visits us, we always try to leave with a thought that they could "bring home" a "gift" as "souvenir" ranging from informational materials to drawings and gadgets made by the children themselves. Last year, for example, we created medals with the school logo. I can still see the surprise and gratitude on the girls' faces as we handed out the medals, demonstrating their appreciation for the children's commitment. This showed us that they fully understood the meaning and, even more, the sentimental and emotional value that those gifts wanted to communicate.

As a teacher, I can say that the experience with the UGA project has always enriched me a little bit more, making me understand that the educational and the relationship value of our school has a great importance. These meetings between cultures are highly constructive, and bring about an understanding of how much knowledge, humanity, culture, sensitivity and emotions can live in both school and children.

Note

1. Davide Vernia, Teacher, Modena Municipal Preschools.

CHAPTER TWENTY-TWO

Starting a Tradition

ELSA FRIGNANI, ANNA MASELLI, AND
FRANCESCA DRAGHICCHIO[1]

It is a great pleasure for us to witness with the following lines the great opportunity that our school had nine years ago when we first met the young teachers from UGA. At that time, we were the first secondary school in Modena chosen by the Victoria Language and Culture team to host foreign university students during their academic year. Together with Roberta Rinaldi and her qualified staff, we exchanged ideas, planned lessons, and brought the American language and its culture to Calvino Secondary School.

All the students who have worked with us succeeded in creating a large motivation and curiosity about their presence in the school. Italian students, teachers, and janitors want to be introduced to them and are always ready to cooperate to make them feel in a familiar environment.

The American students come into our classrooms as "silent observers" and are quickly able to create a profitable, empathetic attitude towards what is going on around them. We never feel language barriers among us and, when necessary, we can always find a way to understand one another. When we realize that they strongly believe in the experience, it becomes easier for us to cooperate with them. We learn that they are eager and proud to answer our innumerable questions, to let us know values of their own culture and country, and to put their teacher education into practice outside of American schools. They want to experience the differences that lie in international schooling and to see the benefits of other teacher educational programs and practices. Most of them get involved in every planned activity and help us with our daily lessons. They are able to apply their own competencies and to assess our students' ways of learning. We widely appreciate their large contribution at the end of each year and look forward to the following year with a new group. As mentor teachers, we have realized that the experience leaves our Italian students more self-confident, more willing to speak, ready to express themselves freely, and willing to take risks. During their stay, we have opportunities to exchange profitable ideas, to share opinions, and to receive and give advice.

For example, a shared geometry lesson was planned a few years ago. The UGA student accepted the proposal of one of our math teachers to compare two different ways of teaching the formulas of the areas of the triangle and the rectangle in one of our second classes. Our students were excited. First, we asked them to draw the two geometrical figures, then both teachers used part of the blackboard to show the different teaching procedures at the same time, focusing the students' attention on the dissimilarities of the two teaching methods. It was very interesting to discuss and analyze the differences in solving problems, as well as all the peculiarities and pros and cons of the two approaches. As a result, we really appreciated the good opportunity offered and the positive attitude together with an increase in the motivation and attention of our students in facing a new way of teaching. We all hope that our school will continue to be a part of this lasting, worthwhile, project.

Note

1. Elsa Frignani, Anna Maselli, and Francesca Draghicchio, Teachers, Calvino Middle School, Istituto Comprehensivo Modena 2.

CHAPTER TWENTY-THREE

A Jewel of a Relationship

IVANA NOBLER[1]

My first meeting with Roberta Rinaldi took place last school year after I had become the Principal of the former *Direzione Didattica 8 di Modena* and after having spent twenty years teaching English at primary schools in *Campania*, my region of origin.

I immediately understood the importance of renewing our collaboration with the Cultural Association *Victoria Language and Culture* to continue to profit from a lively and functioning union, especially in regards to the *UGA/Modena Schools* project. This program, in addition to enhancing the development of our young students' linguistic competencies, helps them broaden their cultural horizons through the relationships they can build with the American students. Indeed, as I had the opportunity to personally verify last year, the American students, using their own style, personality, and skills put themselves into the game in an empathically constructive and balanced manner according to our children's cognitive and emotional intelligence. I consider this exchange program to be a real diamond for our school system. Both American students and Italian students benefit immensely from this cultural exchange.

Note

1. Ivana Nobler, Principal, Comprehensivo Modena 7.

CHAPTER TWENTY-FOUR

Leading the Way

ROBERTA RINALDI AND ANNA GIOVANNINI[1]

Our association, *Victoria Language and Culture*, helped develop and continues to manage a very successful and unique program, which is known in our community as *UGA/Modena Schools*. The program started in 2009 when Dr. Ronald Butchart and Dr. Beth Tolley chaperoned the first group of UGA college students to Modena, in northern Italy.

Our region, Emilia Romagna, is home to the University of Bologna, the oldest university in Europe. It is rich in both beautiful medieval and renaissance cities, with theatres, museums, and cultural events. This area is famous for its cuisine and food products, such as Parma ham, Parmiggian-Reggiano cheese, balsamic vinegar, lasagna, and tortellini to name a few. Close by cities like Verona, Florence, Venice, and Milan area easy to reach and enjoy. Icing on the cake, Emilia Romagna is the home region of a very special, child centered approach to education and schooling. Preschools and elementary schools in particular are well known all over the world for their pedagogy, based on this Reggio approach.

Victoria Language and Culture has been working in the field of cultural exchanges for more than 25 years. We, the founders, Roberta Rinaldi and Anna Giovannini, have devoted our careers to the creation of many programs aimed to raise cross-cultural awareness, mutual understanding, personal growth as well as mastering foreign languages. We pride ourselves on having partners from all over the world; Australia, New Zealand, Germany, England, Hungary, Serbia,

Montenegro, Canada, Mexico, and, of course, the United States. Our programs serve a variety of people and needs. We organize international summer camps for children and teens, academic exchange programs for high school and college students, various experiences for au pairs, schools, and universities. The UGA/Modena Schools Program and the collaboration with Dr. Tolley, who in these past nine years has been a valuable and irreplaceable partner, has helped us and our community strengthen a bond with the United States in an atmosphere or mutual and growing respect, friendliness, cultural understanding, and collaboration.

Briefly, through this program, college students can spend nearly one month in the city of Modena. They work with Italian teachers and interact with children and teens in preschools, elementary, and middle schools. Not only do they have the opportunity to observe the Italian everyday school routine and shadow the Italian teachers, but also to actively participate in class activities and have their own teaching time with the children. They become part of their host schools, but also a special member of their respective Italian families. Modena families welcome the UGA students like real family members, who are involved in their everyday family life and have the opportunity to live as local people do. Their experiences go far beyond those of a tourist. The enthusiasm of both families and students lead to lifelong friendships. In summer 2016, for instance, three Modena families went to Georgia for their American "daughters" weddings. These relationships between the American students and the Italian families are so strong that they often have an impact on the Italian sisters and brothers' future lives. The Italian families' children get to peek inside the American culture and are so inspired by their American college student that they often wish to go and study in the US, either during the summer or for longer programs, and with strong determination try to make their dreams come true. Furthermore, this program allows UGA education majors to witness how the pedagogy is implemented in Italy from a variety of aspects, since family and schools are the most important pillars of the educational system.

Overall, the students' exposure to Italian culture and to an innovative child centered education system provides the participants with a memorable and intense cross-cultural and professional experience. This is extremely beneficial also for all Modena people involved in the program, as well as everybody else, with whom students, teachers, and families share their experiences and their reflections, both in the States and in Italy. Even after nine years, people keep reporting how much they learned about the States and how much they enjoyed sharing their homes and everyday life with their American members of the family. Italian teachers, too, feel that the experience brings new energy to their work and are longing for the chance to one-day visit American schools. All this is very rewarding!

On concluding, the UGA students experience Italian school and family life firsthand, in a safe and caring environment, which encourages all the participants, both American and Italian, to broaden their horizons, share their knowledge, while taking the challenge to adapt to living with people of a different culture. Thanks to living together and through conversations and experiences at home, school, and in the community, the people involved in this program, united by their shared passion for children and education, can experience how close together "worlds apart" can really be. We are very appreciative, happy, and proud to host this program in the Modena community and hope to continue this successful and valuable collaboration with the University of Georgia by welcoming many other UGA groups in the future. Each year this amazing program grows stronger in its influence and continues to afford all participants unexpected lessons from what they didn't see coming.

Note

1. Roberta Rinaldi and Anna Giovannini, Owerns/Directors, Victoria Language and Culture.

Epilogue

This collection of testimonials serves to document the unexpected outcomes of study abroad cultural experiences during the month-long UGA/Modena Schools Study Abroad Program in Modena, Italy. It highlights the value of such experiences and the throng of interwoven dynamics. It showcases the educational learning opportunities for those who participate and how their teacher preparation is enhanced. Its most valuable aspect, however, is the illumination of those dynamics that caught all participants unaware—unaware of cultural similarities and differences, unaware of the power of relationships, unaware of the intricacies of language, and mostly, unaware of themselves. It underscores all of the dynamics that they didn't see coming. The first notions of these realizations are sparked during a celebratory evening when students invite family, friends, and teachers to a final event in order to share what the experience has meant to them. The night is mixed with laughter, tears, hugs, and moments for creating additional lasting memories. Students prepare a brief message of thanks to deliver, and many fail to convey their gratitude without choked words or cracking voices. It is a night of high emotions and a time when many students become aware of the full impact of their Italian experience and the realization that the experience has been life changing.

From the learned experiences and life lessons that came without notice and fanfare, emerge new lessons. The ripples begun in Modena spread widely and continuously and serve as more critical and enhanced lenses for new experiences, as well as for the common day-to-day routines and responsibilities. Unknowingly they were absorbed in "the process of establishing informed and affective connections with other human beings, of thinking and feeling with them at some emotionally, intellectually, and socially significant level, while always remembering that such connections are complicated by sociohistorial forces" (DeStigter, 1999, p. 240). All participants, American students and Italian partners, as well, are left with "an appreciation of global diversity and of human solidarity at an international scale" (Kinginger, 2008, p. 105).

For me the program has moved beyond the opportunity for my own travel experiences and adventures and evolved into an immeasurable privilege of witnessing the awe and excitement of students as they absorb cultural dynamics, learn to navigate strange waters, and see the world with new eyes. It is a time I treasure for reuniting with Italian friends and catching up with the events of their lives. Over the nine years Roberta, Anna, and I have shared our stories of motherhood and the growing pains of our children and now find ourselves shaking our heads in disbelief of how quickly the time has passed and swell with pride in knowing that Emanuele, Sara, Rebecca, and Spencer are now successful adults. What I never saw coming during those stressful early days of reorganizing the program was that motherhood has its own language and international bonds. I am reminded of an incident during the first year when Roberta and her husband traveled several hours to attend Emanuele's fencing competition only to get there and find out that the coach had failed to add him to the lineup. As I watched Roberta "discuss" the situation with the coach I commented to my host mom from that year that I certainly didn't understand Italian but I was fluent in "upset mom".

I also welcome each year the opportunity to meet new families and teachers, reunite with former ones, and offer them my appreciation for their support and for contributing such vital roles to the program. I walk the cobble streets, continue to gasp at the beauty of my surroundings, and immerse myself into the city that for one month each year becomes my home.

In my role as the program director I envision students certainly more prepared to be effective and caring teachers and citizens. More importantly, I picture students better prepared and more willing to embrace and honor differences, including their own. I reflect on the comment made by a student in one of our weekly seminars as she explained that she understood that neither her American ways of doing nor the Italian ways of doing was the better way ... they were just different ways. "Inevitably, students exploring other cultures confront resources, values, and meanings that contradict their habitual assumptions: A great deal depends on how they react to such conflict" (Kinginger, 2008,

p. 12). By reacting positively to challenging experiences, my students improve their opportunities of developing strong social networks with their Italian hosts, thereby opening themselves to learning (Isabelli-Garcia, 2006). While it is argued that short-term study abroad opportunities can possibly "reinforce stereotypes and hasty generalizations" (Cain & Zarate, 1996, p. 68), I hope for students who are less likely to stereotype and assume. I encourage openness and a "willingness to relativize one's own values, beliefs, and behaviors … to be able to see how they might look from an outsider's perspective" (Byram, Gribkova, & Starkey, 2002, p. 12).

I envision young adults who make connections to all of their Italian experiences and transfer the facets of those experiences to new challenges and celebrations. I hope that most, if not all, continue to practice my "48 hour rule" which requires a 48-hour period before making judgments and assessments of people, practices, and circumstances. In our current world of sudden access, immediate responses, and instant evaluations, I am hopeful that the practice of absorbing and thinking through information before reacting has proven its merits to my student participants. Bennett (2010) found that students participating in a study abroad experience "were more appreciative of the complexity of US American life, and thus less likely to engage in stereotyping. I do not believe a single student would have judged the experience a waste of time" (p. 419).

As director I reflect, too, on the impact the experience has had on our Italian families and teachers. My students and I are ambassadors for the American culture and take that responsibility seriously. Interactions with us are more often than not an initial introduction to the USA for our Italian hosts. To establish and leave an admirable impression of America and ourselves is paramount during the program and beyond. I remind students that they represent the teacher education programs of our college, the University of Georgia, the United States, and most importantly, themselves, and the impressions left should be favorable ones. Bellah (1985) in *Habits of the Heart* laments his deep concern about the deterioration of social capital and civic engagement in American character. Through my nine years of directing the UGA/Modena Schools program, I feel confident that the cross cultural experiences organized, planned and included in the program serve to ignite in my students a sense of social capital and civic engagement that continues with them long after they return to their normal lives and routines. Documentation of such notions, both explicit and implicit, is evident throughout each chapter of the book.

Each September I begin a new round of recruitment for the program, although each year it becomes easier due to the word of mouth of former participants. They are certainly the best ambassadors of the program. As I plan for year #10 so many memories and anecdotes from the former years come to mind, and I anticipate with excitement the additional memories and anecdotes that this year will bring. I shake my head in disbelief of how the program has progressed since those days of digging up any and all information I could find to revive it. Its success and impact offer authentic examples of what hard work and determination can accomplish.

I think back to my initial trip to Italy to meet the associates of Victoria Language and Culture for the first time and to work with them to put the final details of the program into place. I vividly recall my labored interactions with taxi drivers in Genoa, relying on a clock and a printed schedule (numbers are universal) to purchase train tickets from the agent in Milan, and realizing the frequency of short-term shop closings in every town and city so that proprietors could go for "caffe." Whenever I reflect on such times I am reminded that regardless of the awkwardness, the lack of language, or the wash of frustration, I managed. I negotiated my hour-long taxi tour through Genoa. I purchased the correct tickets to Verona and Venice. I returned a short while later to purchase the item I had seen in the closed shop window. Somehow I knew that hand-scribbled note on the shop door meant, "will be back soon."

I am the child in Whitman's poem who went forth. Nine years later it is as Whitman wrote. Those things I saw became part of me "for the day or a certain part of the day … or for many years or stretching cycles of years (Whitman, 1855, p. 118). They have helped make me who I am as a person and as the director of a valuable study abroad program in Modena, Italy. My students and I will continue to go forth and absorb all that we can from this treasured intercultural experience. There is still so much out there that none of us see coming.

References

Bellah, R. N. (1985). *Habits of the heart: Individualism and commitment in American life.* Berkeley: University of California Press.

Bennett, M. J. (2010). A short conceptual history of intercultural learning in study abroad. In W. Hoffa, & S. Depaul (Eds.), *A history of U. S. study abroad: 1965–present.* Special publication of *Frontiers: The Interdisciplinary Journal of Study Abroad*, pp. 419–449.

Byram, M., Gribkova, B., & Starkey, H. (2002). *Developing the intercultural dimension in language teaching: A practical introduction for teacher.* Council of Europe. Retrieved from http://lrc.cornell.edu/director/intercultural.pdf

Cain, A., & Zarate, G. (1996). The role of training courses in developing openness to otherness: From tourism to ethnography. *Language, Culture, and Curriculum, 9*(1), 66–83.

DeStigter, T. (1999). Public displays of affection: Political community through critical empathy. *Research in the Teaching of English, 33*(3), 235–244.

Isabelli-Garcia, C. (2006). Study abroad social networks, motivation and attitudes: Implications for second language acquisition. In M. A. Duron & E. Churchill (Eds.), *Language learners in study abroad contexts* (pp. 231–258). Clevedon, UK: Multilingual Matters.

Kinginger, C. (2008). Language learning in study abroad: Case studies of Americans in France. *Modern Language Journal, 92*, 1–124.

Whitman, W. (1855). *Leaves of grass.* Originally published 1855. ©2009 Sam Torode. Americanrenaissancebooks.com

About the Contributors

Shelly Gleaton Blair participated in the program in 2013. She currently lives in Monroe, Georgia, which is right outside of Athens and teaches kindergarten in Walton County, where she attended school as a child. She has gone on to receive her gifted teaching endorsement and is currently enrolled in an Education Specialist program for Curriculum and Instruction. Shelly returned to Modena to work with Roberta and Victoria Language and Culture for the 2014 Summer English Camp in Modena, as well as 2015 Summer English Camp in Soliera. She stayed with the Ferraris, her host family both times. She also returned in June 2013 with her parents in order for them to meet the Ferraris. She married in 2016 and her Italian host sister attended the wedding. Shelly's Italian experience ignited in her a desire to see more of the world. She has since traveled around the United Arab Emirates (visiting Dubai and Abu Dhabi), Spain, Portugal, France, England, Morocco, and many places in the Caribbean and Central America. She and her husband plan on returning to visit the Ferraris in Modena and traveling around Italy.

Sarah Erdman participated in the UGA/Modena Schools Study Abroad Program in the 2016. She graduated in December 2017 from the University of Georgia with a degree in early childhood education. Her next career plans are to pursue a masters degree. Almost immediately after returning from Italy Sarah was already planning a return to Modena. In the summer of 2017 she and her mom traveled to Italy and were greeted with open arms and many tears at the Bologna Airport by her Italian host mother. She reports that she and her host family picked up right where they left off and strengthened their bond even further, something she didn't even think was possible. The 5 days spent together were filled with more hugs, happy tears, and laughter. Like her host mom says, "It's not goodbye...it's see you later." Sarah is already looking forward to and planning her next visit to Modena, a place she now calls home.

Bethany McLaughlin Doan participated in the Modena study abroad program in 2011. After teaching for three years in Atlanta upon graduation from UGA in 2013, she moved to Richmond, Virginia where she currently teaches high school English. Throughout her teaching career she has directed two student study abroad programs traveling to Germany, England, Ireland, and Prague inspiring students to explore and broadened their horizons as the UGA program first instilled in her. She reports that on her own she has traveled again to Italy, re-living her past experiences of gelato and pizza. In 2015, she backpacked through Europe visiting France, England, Spain, and Italian islands of Cinque Terre. Bethany asserts that the study abroad program was a catalyst not only for the passion towards her teaching career as she witnessed first hand the universality of language, but also a passion for traveling, broadening her horizons, and exploring the unknown in an effort to continually improve herself and her appreciation for others as she continues to venture outside her comfort zone in foreign countries.

Ha-Young (Gloria) Yu participated in the Modena Study Abroad program in May 2015. This experience inspired Gloria to pursue a teaching career, which let her to apply to the Master of Arts in Teaching for Early Childhood Education program at the University of Georgia. She graduated from this program in the fall of 2017. Gloria lives with her mom in Marietta, Georgia. Last summer, Gloria and her family traveled for about a month to South Korea and Vietnam, and she hopes to return to Modena soon.

Jordan Moore participated in the Modena Study Abroad Program in May of 2017. She graduated in December 2017 from the University of Georgia with a Master of the Arts of Teaching degree in Early Childhood Education. After graduating, she moved to Maryland to live and work part-time at a summer camp and retreat center while searching for a teaching position. Her trip to Italy was her first time traveling to Europe, and she plans on returning in early 2018 to travel around Europe and visit her Italian family. She is hopeful it will be the first of many return trips as she continues to build a life-long friendship with her Italian family.

The Ferrari Family, Fabrizio, Anna, Cecilia and Francesco, hosted students in 2012 and 2013. They decided to host because they think these experiences enrich their family greatly and create new opportunities of growth and knowledge. They have maintained communication with their American daughters, even sending their own daughter Cecilia to the states to attend the wedding of one.

The Corciolani Family, Elena, Laura, and Piero, have hosted American students from 2009 to 2016. They decided to host because they think this experience gives their family the opportunity to grow from a cultural, linguistic and also human point of view, and to compare their ideas, habits and cuisines with those different from their own

Camilla Giovanardi has hosted an American student in her classroom twice … once in first grade and the other in fourth grade. Both times she was very happy about the experience.

She holds a degree in Foreign Languages and Modern Literature. She has been teaching in elementary schools since 1995. She passed the exam to teach English in middle and high schools, but younger children are her real passion. She is also coordinator for other classes and for the English commission of the Comprensivo Modena 7 (a group of 4 elementary schools and 1 middle school that share an administrator and). Camilla and her colleague Stefania Lancellotti decided to host the UGA American students because they believe this is a complete experience from all points of view: not only the language but above all an opportunity to grow personally and to build important and deep human relations.

Stefania Lancellotti has welcomed American students twice, both as a host mom and as a host teacher and was thrilled about the experience. She graduated in Pedagogy at the University of Bologna in 1994 and she immediately started to teach in elementary schools. She passed the exam to teach Philosophy and Human Sciences in high schools, and she obtained the school counselor title in 2008. She has served as a collaborator with the school principal for eight years. Together with a colleague she has taken on the responsibility of school coordination, of parents' committee relations management, and she is involved in reading-writing projects. From 1999 to 2001 she worked as a pedagogue to support the schools in her Comprensivo.

Elsa Frignani has hosted American students in her classroom since the beginning of the program. She has been teaching English for 40 years, and also taking care of students with special needs. For three years she shared, with a colleague of the Calvino Middle School, the role of Special Projects Teacher, for the inclusion of disadvantaged children. For ten years she has taken on the responsibility of some afternoon projects like 'compiti insieme' (homework together) and laboratories in collaboration with 'Città e scuola' of Modena.

Anna Maselli has hosted seven American students in her classroom. She has been teaching for 25 years. She began teaching in elementary schools and currently is an English teacher in middle schools.

Francesca Draghicchio has three American students in her classroom. She has been an English teacher for 20 years. She also worked for 5 years in elementary schools as special teacher of English and 8 years teaching English to adults (from 16 to 70 years old). The teachers of Calvino Middle School believe that this is a unique opportunity for their students and for the teachers, too, to compare new ways of teaching.

Ivana Nobler has worked in the school system since 1991. From 1991 to 1994 she was a high school teacher, and from 1995 to 2014 she taught English in elementary schools. In 2015 she became the principal of the Comprensivo Modena 7. Her schools have hosted American students since the beginning of the program. She believes it is a great opportunity to broaden the cultural horizons of all involved through the relationships formed between the American students and the Italian children and teachers. They consider this exchange program to be a real diamond for their schools.

Concetta Ponticelli has been the principal of the Comprensivo Modena 1 (a group of 1 preschool, 3 elementary schools, and 1 middle school that share an administrator) for four years. She has also hosted five American students in her home. Before becoming a principal she worked as an English teacher in high schools. Her schools decided to host UGA American students because she and the teachers believe it is an enriching experience for everyone. They feel that the program shows how teaching and learning does not pass only through words but also through hearts.

Sara Lorenzini has served as a host teacher for the American students for 9 years. She has been teaching in elementary schools for 20 years. She was a religion teacher and for one year taught at "Stella Maris", a special school that is part of the University of Pisa. She has also been vice principal, and she is collaborating with the University of Modena and Reggio Emilia on science projects. She thinks hosting American students in her classroom is a great opportunity to grow from a personal and professional point of view. She describes the American students as enthusiastic and motivated and feels the experience offers a breath of fresh air for everyone.

Benedetta Pantoli The schools under Benedetta's administration have hosted UGA American students since 2010. From 1990 to 2008 she was in charge of the Education and Rehabilitation Area of a social co-operative. For four of those years she worked as a Pedagogical Coordinator. Since September 2008 she is the person in charge of all the age 0–6 schools of Modena Municipality.

Davide Vernia has been teaching English in Modena Municipal Pre-Schools since 1997. From 2000 to 2013 he worked at MoMo, an educational center for children located in the heart of Modena, which welcomes children from ages 1–11 and offers three different services: nursery (ages 0–3), game center (ages 2–5) and laboratories/workshops (ages 6–11). He has hosted American students since 2010, both in his pre-school classroom and during their visits to MoMo. He thinks it is an important opportunity to get to know new foreign future teachers, compare different teaching approaches and build deep human relations.

Roberta Rinaldi and **Anna Giovannini** are the owners and directors of Victoria Language and Culture. They have been working with cultural exchange programs and involved with the teaching of English since 1991. For many years Roberta and Anna taught English to children, teens and adults. They have been managing the work of Victoria Language and Culture for over 25 years. In addition to coordinating study abroad programs for college students, they also arrange and oversee the cultural exchanges of high school students in the United States, in many European countries, and in Australia. They also arrange the placement of aupairs and organize a successful English summer camp program for Italian children utilizing the skills of mother-tongue American students to work as counselors at the camp.

Emily Gwaltney participated in the Modena Study Abroad Program in May of 2016. She is continuing her studies at the University of Georgia and currently works as an intern at the UGA Wesley Foundation where she helps facilitate a mentoring program for children in Athens and for UGA students. She lives in Athens, and has not yet returned to Italy but has no doubts that she will return in the near future. Emily feels that studying and teaching in Modena was one of the best decisions she made during her college career.

Kelli Lewis Daniels participated in the UGA study abroad program during Maymester 2010 while working on her MED in early childhood education. She has been teaching third grade for seven years, and currently teaches at a charter school, The Academy for Classical Education, located in middle Georgia. She lives in Forsyth, Ga., with her husband, their twin girls, and their dog. Since studying abroad she has visited Mexico and The Dominican Republic, and hopes to travel back to Italy one day with her family. Since returning from her study abroad experience, she has kept in touch with her Italian host family through occasional email exchanges and Instagram. She keeps photos of her Italian family and her Italian class in her third grade classroom.

Zarina Maude Wafula graduated from the University of Georgia with a Masters in Early Childhood/Elementary Education in May 2017. She also received certification to teach STEAM and Gifted Education. She grew up in Kenya, and she loves to teach, learn new things, explore the outdoors and spend time with family and friends. After graduating, she relocated back to Kenya where she teaches STEM, KiSwahili and Library at Woodland Star International School. Nothing has challenged her as much as being a teacher. She is a strong proponent of Hundred Languages of Children (Reggio Emilia), and believes that there are a hundred different ways of thinking, of discovering, and of learning.

Taylor York participated in the UGA/Modena Schools study abroad program in 2015 and graduated from the University of Georgia with her bachelor and master's degrees in Early Childhood Education in Summer 2017. She returned to Modena with the program in 2017 as a graduate assistant. After graduation she moved to Atlanta and currently teaches fourth grade. She stays in touch with her Italian family and friends and has every intention of returning to Modena soon.

Megan Elyse Greene participated in the UGA/Modena Schools study abroad program in 2015. She graduated from the University of Georgia with bachelor and master degrees in Early Childhood Education in May 2017. She feels that her study abroad program is a highlight of her college experience. Teaching English and working at the VLC camp inspired her to complete her English as a second or other language (ESOL) endorsement and to pursue a teaching position at a diverse school post-graduation. She currently teaches third grade math at a year-round, Title I school in Washington, DC. She stays in regular contact with her Italian host family hopes to return to Modena in the future.

Rachel Miller McKee participated in the Modena study abroad program in 2013. She is currently a second grade teacher in Athens, GA, enjoying life with her husband and their two dogs. Studying abroad convinced her to further her teaching training, and she currently is working towards a specialist degree in curriculum and instruction. Since participating in the UGA/Modena Schools study abroad program, she has returned two times to work in the Victoria Language and Culture summer camp, spend time with her Italian families, and travel. The study abroad experience opened up her world to traveling and has led her to explore all over Italy as well as Paris, London, Barcelona, Mexico, Costa Rica and the Maldives!

Tatyanna Vincenty never thought that she would travel outside the Eastern Time Zone, let alone outside of the country. She was one of the last applicants to sign up for the UGA/Modena Schools study abroad experience and will be forever grateful to Dr. Tolley for allowing her in after the deadline. She graduated from the University of Georgia with two degrees in Early Childhood Education and still considers her time in Italy as one of the most important aspects of her education. She has been hired to teach in Cobb County, Georgia, but her Italian *bimbi* will never be forgotten.

Chelsea Lynne Walker, M.Ed., CF-SLP, is a pediatric speech-language pathologist in Columbus, Georgia, treating children in a school setting as well as a private practice. Chelsea graduated from the University of Georgia with her bachelor of science in education degree in 2015 and is a 2017 graduate of the University of Georgia's Communication Sciences and Disorders master's program. Chelsea is the immediate past president of the National Student Speech-Language-Hearing Association and continues to be passionate about growing future leaders in her profession. She also continues to value the experiences she had in Italy.

Natalia Prada-Rey Cooper studied Early Childhood Education at UGA and studied abroad in Modena, Italy during the summers of 2009 and 2010. Her experiences in Italy had a major impact on her life and career today. After graduation, Natalia got her Master's in Education from Vanderbilt University. She taught third grade for three years and now works as an Educational Consultant at Peabody College. She lives in Nashville, Tennessee with her husband and golden retriever, and they have a baby boy on the way! She remains in contact with her host family in Modena and plans to return with her family soon.

Index

reaction to study abroad students, xviii,
  12–13, 22–23, 38, 49, 52, 59, 91,
  97–99, 108
Italian teachers
  benefits to, 30, 90, 97–98, 99–100,
    104–05, 107, 110
  fears of, 29, 38, 99
  reaction to study abroad students, 12, 38,
    49, 70, 89–91, 99, 103–04, 106

J

jetlag. *See* exhaustion

L

language barrier, xiii, 12, 22, 24, 29–30, 37,
  48–50, 53, 59, 65, 76, 78, 85, 94, 104, 106
language barrier coping strategies, 12, 23,
  38, 40, 48–49, 53, 59, 66, 91
long-term effects of program, 3–4, 45–46

M

Maranello, 42
materialism, 16–17, 23, 66
meetings before departure, xviii, 92–93
meetings in Italy, xiii, 59, 76, 84, 114
Milan, xiv, 12, 25, 31, 35, 41, 83, 93, 109, 116
Modena description, xii, 37–38, 40, 42, 56,
  84, 90, 109
Murano, 41

N

non-verbal communication, xii, 12, 22, 38,
  47–48, 50, 52–53, 59, 65–66, 73, 78, 80,
  83, 96

P

Parma, 40, 109
personal issues, 9–10, 11, 13
Pisa, 84, 88
placement in homes, xii, xvii, 51
placement in schools, xviii, 29–30
preparation for trip, xii–xiii, xviii

R

Ravenna, 41
reasons for studying abroad, 11, 13, 21, 26,
  58, 87, 92
Reggio Emilia method, xii–xiii, xv–xvi,
  xviii–xix, 45, 51–53, 55, 59, 64, 109
relationships with
  host family, xvii–xviii, 12–13,
    16–17, 22, 26–27, 34–35,
    51–52, 60, 62–64, 77, 82–83,
    95, 110
  Italian students, 12–13, 17, 22,
    23, 26, 38, 49, 65–66, 73–74,
    95, 98
  Italian teachers, 12, 38, 49, 52, 74
  other study abroad students, 13, 16, 38,
    40–41, 76, 84
Rome, 32, 81, 84, 93

S

second language acquisition, xvi, 52–54, 80
study abroad program
Subtleties, 4, 87–88

T

themes of book, 4

U

V